AF334897

RICHARD AND ANNE

A Play in Two Acts

RICHARD AND ANNE

A Play in Two Acts

by

MAXWELL ANDERSON

with an Introduction and Notes by

ROXANE C. MURPH

and Two Letters from

ROBERT SHERWOOD

McFarland & Company, Inc., Publishers
Jefferson, North Carolina, and London

Frontispiece: **Maxwell Anderson, photograph by Vandamm Studio, New York, courtesy of Mrs. Maxwell Anderson**

British Library Cataloguing-in-Publication data are available

Library of Congress Cataloguing-in-Publication Data

Anderson, Maxwell, 1888–1959.
    Richard and Anne : a play in two acts / by Maxwell Anderson.
      p. cm.
    Includes bibliographical references.
    ISBN 0-89950-803-0 (lib. bdg. : 55# alk. paper) ∞
    1. Richard III, King of England, 1452–1485 — Drama.   2. Anne,
Queen, consort of Richard III, King of England, 1456–1485 — Drama.
I. Title.
PS3501.N256R53   1995
812'.52 — dc20   94-37326
                                                               CIP

Manufactured in the United States of America

McFarland & Company, Inc., Publishers
  Box 611, Jefferson, North Carolina 28640

Table of Contents

Introduction
(Roxane C. Murph)

Maxwell Anderson was a dominant force in the American theater for more than two decades, and when he died on February 28, 1959, he left behind a large body of work, which included more than thirty published plays, a volume of poetry, two collections of essays, and twenty unfinished or unpublished plays. One of those completed but unpublished works was *Richard and Anne*, a two-act verse play about Richard III and Anne Neville, his wife.

Despite his avid interest in British and European history, as evidenced by several of his best known plays, such as *Elizabeth the Queen* and *Joan of Lorraine*, Anderson was the quintessential American playwright, both by upbringing and philosophy. Although he lived in New York for most of his creative writing career, his roots and his heart were in middle America. He was born in Atlantic, Pennsylvania, on December 15, 1888, the son of a peripatetic Baptist minister who moved his family frequently during the years of Maxwell's childhood. Anderson attended public schools in Pennsylvania, Ohio, Iowa, and North Dakota, and graduated from the University of North Dakota in 1911. He received an M.A. degree from Stanford University in 1914, and taught there and at Whittier College in California. Anderson was fired from Whittier, a Quaker institution, for his anti-war views, and got his revenge in *Valley Forge* and *Knickerbocker Holiday*, two plays in which he satirized this supposedly pacifist sect.

Anderson's political views continued to get him into trouble after he had quit teaching and gone into editorial writing, and he was fired from one paper for questioning Germany's ability to pay reparations after World War I. He wrote editorials for two San Francisco newspapers before leaving for New York and a job on *The New Republic*. In May 1919 he joined the staff of *The New York Globe* and then went to *The New York World*, where he worked with Deems Taylor, Alexander Woolcott, and Franklin P. Adams.

In a 1956 interview with Louis M. Starr, Anderson noted that while working for *The World* he had refused to write about politics, a subject he claimed did not interest him. As a result he ended up writing "all the decorative editorials, about the flowers, the human interest things. I wasn't worrying about politics." When the editors realized that Anderson would never become the kind of editor they wanted, they hired Walter Lippmann to replace him.[1]

Despite his disclaimer, Anderson obviously developed an interest in government and politics, and these themes appear in some form in many of his plays and other writings. *Both Your Houses*, which earned Anderson the Pulitzer Prize for drama in 1933, is a powerful satire showing how power corrupts, even in a democratic constitutional government. It was, wrote critic John Mason Brown, "as merciless and disheartening a picture of governmental corruption as anyone could imagine. It is a shocking, bitter indictment, calculated to raise doubts in the hearts of even the staunchest supporters of the democratic ideal."[2] Although the play was written during the Hoover administration, it was not produced until Roosevelt was in office, and Anderson may have hoped that the new government would correct some of the abuses he had satirized.[3] His thesis that graft and corruption are endemic in government is one that he returned to in other works.

Knockerbocker Holiday, another play with a political theme, and one of his most successful, is a satire of Roosevelt's New Deal, written at a time when both the president and his policies were enormously popular with the public, if not always with writers. In 1938 Anderson felt compelled to explain his position in a preface to the published edition of the play, which is set in New Amsterdam in 1647. Noting that there had been "a good deal of critical bewilderment over the political opinions expressed in the play, and not a little resentment at my definitions of government and democracy," Anderson explained that he was only reflecting the general feelings of the country at the time of the American Revolution. "At that time," he added, "it was generally believed, as I believe now, that the gravest and most constant danger to a man's life, liberty and happiness is the government under which he lives."[4]

Anderson went on to warn against the too great concentration of power in the hands of a few, and the danger that this country could, by inaugurating such programs as Social Security, end up in the same condition as Russia, Germany, and Italy, all then ruled by dictators. No matter how noble the goal of these social programs, which aimed at protecting the citizens from economic hardship, "it can have but one result, the loss of individual liberty in thought, speech and action."[5] The views that Anderson expressed both in the preface to *Knickerbocker Holiday* and the play itself were modified by the advent of war, when he realized that government must impose some restrictions upon the liberty of its citizens in times of danger. In a talk he gave on November 20, 1938, during an intermission of the performance of the play, he expressed his willingness to compromise that much for the sake of democracy.[6]

Anderson had started writing plays in college, and these early works, which used Elizabethan devices of verse dialogue and songs, prefigured his later history plays. His great love of music is evident in plays like *Truckline Cafe* (1946), for which he composed one of the songs, and in the fact that he wrote the libretti for *Knickerbocker Holiday*, which included the still popular "September Song," and *Lost in the Stars*, for both of which his close friend and neighbor Kurt Weill wrote the music. In 1950 the two collaborated on a musical version of Mark Twain's *Huckleberry Finn*, entitled *Raft on the River*, with the alternate title *River Chanty*. Weill died before the musical score was completed, and in 1951 Anderson revised the first act in collaboration with Joshua Logan. The playwright tried, unsuccessfully at first, to interest another composer in completing the score, and finally Irving Berlin agreed to do it. Apparently, however, Anderson was displeased with Logan's script changes, and he abandoned the play.[7] "This Time Next Year," one of the songs Weill wrote for this work, is included in a recently recorded collection of the composer's songs.[8]

During the 1930s and 1940s, Anderson's most productive years, he wrote a string of successful plays, including *Elizabeth the Queen* (1930), *Both Your Houses* (1933), *Mary of Scotland* (1933), *Valley Forge* (1934), *Winterset* (1935), *The Wingless Victory* (1936), *High Tor* (1937), *Knickerbocker Holiday* (1938), *Key Largo* (1939), *Joan of Lorraine* (1946), *Anne of the Thousand Days* (1948), and *Lost in the Stars* (1950), a musical adaptation of Alan Paton's novel *Cry the Beloved Country*. Both *Winterset* and *High Tor* earned Drama Critics' Circle awards for Anderson. He wrote several unsuccessful plays as well, not surprising in view of his enormous output. The long dry period that followed these prolific years ended in 1954 when Anderson had great success with his adaptation of William Marsh's novel *The Bad Seed*, but this was his last hit.

Several of these plays were adapted into critically acclaimed and commercially successful films. Burgess Meredith, a close friend of Anderson's, made his screen debut as Mio in *Winterset*, which was inspired by the Sacco-Vanzetti case. The 1936 movie used the original cast of the Broadway play. Three years later Bette Davis and Errol Flynn played the title roles in *Elizabeth and Essex*, the movie based on *Elizabeth the Queen*, Anderson's romanticized version of the love-hate relationship between the queen and her proud, ambitious courtier.

The 1944 film version of *Knickerbocker Holiday* starred Nelson Eddy and Charles Coburn, and in 1948 movies were made of two more Anderson plays. Ingrid Bergman repeated her Broadway role in *Joan of Lorraine* in a movie retitled *Joan of Arc*, with a cast that included Jose Ferrer. *Key Largo*, with Humphrey Bogart, Lauren Bacall, Edward G. Robinson, and Lionel Barrymore, was loosely based on Anderson's play, but the changes wrought in his work, including the typical Hollywood happy ending, destroyed much of its integrity.

Not even Hollywood could save Anne Boleyn from the headsman's axe in the 1969 film version of *Anne of the Thousand Days*, Anderson's moving portrayal of the tragic life of the queen from the year 1526, when she first engaged the king's attention, until 1536 when she met her unhappy end. Genevieve Bujold and Richard Burton played Anne and Henry VIII.

The Bad Seed, Anderson's last successful play, was also one of the most commercially successful movies based on his works. The 1956 film starred Nancy Kelly, with Patty McCormack as surely one of fiction's most evil children. Brock Peters and Melba Moore played leading roles in the 1974 film version of *Lost in the Stars*, Anderson's moving adaptation of Paton's novel.

James Maxwell Anderson was a poet and noted critic as well as a playwright, but poetry was his first love. In a letter to a friend, dated May 4, 1927, he wrote

> I quit teaching because I could make more money in journalism and I quit writing editorials because I could make more in the theater. The only work of mine for which I have much respect is my one volume of verse. What I want more than anything is to successfully put poetry into plays. What the theater needs more than anything else is poetry, and what poetry needs more than anything else is an audience.[9]

Anderson believed passionately that poetry was the proper language for the theater, and that none of the works of even the greatest modern playwrights could compare with the great verse dramas of the past. "Our modern dramatists are not poets," he wrote, "and the best prose in the world is inferior on the stage to the best poetry.... To me it is inescapable that prose is the language of information and poetry the language of emotion."[10] *Winterset* was the first successful modern verse play, and many of Anderson's other plays, like *Elizabeth the Queen* and *Mary of Scotland*, were written either partly or wholly in verse. By 1956, however, when he spoke with Louis M. Starr, Anderson had become discouraged about the public's acceptance of the medium. Modern audiences, he complained, do not accept verse plays easily, and "if you give it to them, you have to trick them or force it down their throats—make them listen by some other device. Because the music of words is a very small part of what people are listening to now.... I think my verse has been disintegrating under the pressure—the pressure of public opinion. They don't want it." Referring to *Anne of the Thousand Days*, he added that it was written in "a sort of ragged verse that you couldn't call blank verse, and partly in prose."[11] Anderson seemed to feel that first the movies and then television were responsible for the public's rejection of verse plays, but he continued to write some of his last works at least partly in verse. In *Richard and Anne*, one of his last works, the historical characters generally speak in verse, while the contemporary sections of the play are mostly in prose.

Despite Maxwell Anderson's reservations about the public's acceptance of his work, the playwright was held in high esteem by contemporary critics, who frequently compared him with Eugene O'Neill. John Gassner, the noted critic, author, and for many years the chairman of the play department of the Theatre Guild, and professor of English, comparative literature, and drama at Columbia and Yale universities, declares that "Maxwell Anderson's candidacy for this honor has been supported by his capacity for pungent prose and winged utterance. To these he has added not only a gift of humor and theatrical effect but a sensitive and questioning intellect.... Almost alone in the American theatre since O'Neill, he has attempted to rise beyond the pedestrian realistic drama. He has tried to scale the forbidding peaks of poetic composition by means of a pliant and free blank verse, and he has even leaped into the stratosphere of fantasy. He has, above all, striven to make tragedy prevail in the modern theatre. . . ." If he did not always succeed in his aspirations, if he occasionally dealt in generalities, "valid for the spirit but not for the actual realities that he himself stresses by the choice of his themes," he nevertheless "flies high in his poetic style . . . [and] equally high in his statement and resolution of dramatic themes because he wants the spirit to prevail at all costs." If, on occasion, "he flies too high, . . . and therefore violates both the logic of his own situations and the logic of common fact," he nevertheless "has a right to climb or soar, and he is a more considerable artist for it."[12]

Anderson's use of poetry in his works implemented his philosophy of the theater, which he explained in his essay "Off Broadway" (1947):

> The theatrical profession may protest as much as it likes, the theologians may protest, and the majority of those who see our plays would probably be amazed to hear it, but the theater is a religious institution devoted entirely to the exaltation of the spirit of man. It has no formal religion. It is a church without a creed, but there is no doubt in my mind that our theater, instead of being, as the evangelical ministers used to believe, the gateway to hell, is as much a worship as the theater of the Greeks, and has exactly the same meaning in our lives.[13]

"The plays that please most," he added further on in this essay, "and run the longest . . . are representative of human loyalty, courage, love that purges the soul, grief that enobles."

The writer of the March 1, 1959, obituary in *The New York Times* noted that Anderson "looked upon the theatre as the central artistic symbol of the struggle of good and evil within men. Set a man on the stage, he once said, and you knew instantly where he stands morally with the race. The theatre to Mr. Anderson . . . was an affirmation also that men have within themselves the beasts from which they descend and the God toward which they climb."[14]

Anderson's first play, in verse, written in 1923 while he was still working for the *World*, was *White Desert*, and it, like his second play, *A Holy Terror*, which he wrote with George Abbott, was a failure, and neither has been published. Years later, recalling *White Desert*, which ran for a couple of weeks, he remarked, "It was a poetic tragedy, and didn't deserve to last that long. Oh, yes, I felt that way at the time. I didn't know why anybody produced it."[15] His next play, *What Price Glory?*, written in collaboration with Laurence Stallings, was a huge success when it opened at the Plymouth Theater in 1924, and it ran for about four hundred performances on Broadway and on tour. The play, which gives a realistic, nonromanticized view of war unusual at the time, created some controversy, mostly for its uninhibited use of profanity, and there were several unsuccessful attempts by the authorities, both military and civilian, to censor it. *What Price Glory?* was "an inspired ode to the obscenity of war, [which] brought from Heywood Broun the observation that it was the best play about war and possibly 'the best American play about anything.'"[16] With this play Anderson and Stallings had helped to bring more realism to the theater, and its success enabled Anderson to quit the newspaper business and devote full time to writing plays. He and Stallings collaborated on two more plays, *First Flight*, a fictional tale about young Andrew Jackson, which takes place in 18th century North Carolina, and *The Buccaneer*, about the pirate Sir Henry Morgan, which is set in 17th century Panama, and both produced at the Plymouth Theater in 1925. During the following years, as Anderson continued to write plays, he wrote as well a collection of poems entitled *You Who Have Dreams*.

In 1939 Anderson published *The Essence of Tragedy*, the first systematic theory of tragedy by an American playwright. It was written originally as a paper to be read at a session of the Modern Language Association meeting in New York in January 1938, and is included in *Off Broadway*, a collection of essays about the theater. In this work he discusses "discovery," which he calls one of the most important elements of tragedy, and the mainspring in the mechanism of a modern play, in which the hero discovers

> some element in his environment or in his own soul of which he has not been aware — or which he has not taken sufficiently into account.... A play should lead up to and away from a central crisis, and this crisis should consist in a discovery by the leading character which has an indelible effect on his thought and emotion, completely alters his course of action.... It must affect him emotionally, and it must alter his direction in the play.[17]

Richard's actions and emotions in *Richard and Anne* are deeply affected by his realization of how history has portrayed him, and much of the action of the play hinges on this discovery.

In order to appreciate *Richard and Anne*, it is necessary to know something of the background of the War of the Roses, the period in which the characters lived.* Richard III was born on October 2,

*The following brief account of the Wars of the Roses, which has as its focus the part played by Richard Plantagenet as Duke of Gloucester and King Richard III, is based on those facts generally [continued]

1452, in Fotheringhay Castle in Northamptonshire, the twelfth and youngest surviving child of Richard, Duke of York, and his wife Cecily Neville. It was a dangerous time, for the king, Henry VI, a weak, pious man who was subject to periodic bouts of madness, was unable to keep order among his ambitious nobles or in the country at large. Henry had married Margaret of Anjou, the daughter of the penniless, landless King René of Sicily. The marriage was arranged by the Duke of Suffolk, who persuaded Henry to turn over to Margaret's father two English provinces in France. She came to England without a dowry, and had to be supplied with clothes suitable to her new estate by her English friends. The marriage was unpopular with the English, who did not like the French and resented the give-away of English possessions. Although the people loved their monkish king, the arrogant and vengeful queen and her greedy favorites were soon the objects of much hatred and scorn.

The Duke of York, Richard's father, was the leader of the opposition to the queen and her favorites, and her hatred of him and his faction was intense. By 1459 there had been several bloody battles between the Yorkists and Lancastrians, and York, fearing that Fotheringhay was no longer safe, moved his family to Ludlow, his castle on the Welsh Marches. It was there that Richard met his seventeen-year-old brother Edward for the first time. The queen's forces attacked and destroyed Ludlow, and the duke, his two eldest sons, Edward and Edmund, his brother-in-law the Earl of Salisbury, and his nephew the Earl of Warwick, fled abroad. Richard, his brother George, and their mother were put into the custody of the duchess's Lancastrian sister, the Duchess of Buckingham.

York had sailed to Ireland, where he was royally received; Ireland remained loyal to the Yorkist cause long after the death of its last monarch, supporting the claims of both pretenders to Tudor's throne, Lambert Simnel and Perkin Warbeck. Warwick, Salisbury, and Edward had gone to Calais, which had remained loyal to Warwick, its captain. The following June the three men, with a large following,

accepted by historians. The varying interpretations of these facts over the past five hundred years have resulted in a lively and occasionally acrimonious debate regarding the character, actions, and motives of Richard III. As a result, there has been a great deal of speculation about evidence which might have supported one side or the other, but which has been lost or destroyed. For detailed and balanced accounts of the period see Charles Ross, The Wars of the Roses: A Concise History *(London, 1976);* Edward IV *(Berkeley, 1974);* Richard III *(Berkeley, 1981); Paul Murray Kendall,* Richard the Third *(New York, 1956); and P. W. Hammand and Anne F. Sutton,* Richard III: The Road to Bosworth Field *(London, 1985).*

returned to England, where they captured the king, and took over the government. When the Duke of York returned to London, it was to press his claim to the throne, a claim which he and his faction believed to be stronger than that of Henry VI. York was descended from the second son of Edward III, and the Lancastrians from John of Gaunt, the third son. When Henry IV, Gaunt's son, seized the throne from his cousin Richard II, he passed over Roger Mortimer, the legitimate heir, a child at the time, and the ancestor of Richard of York. York's claim, however legitimate it may have been, was not supported even by his own followers, who were interested only in reforming the government, and so, after much legal debate it was agreed that Henry would keep his throne, but that York would be named Protector and heir apparent.

This solution may have been acceptable to most of those concerned, but it enraged the queen, who refused to let her son be set aside in favor of her despised enemy. On December 30, 1460, the queen's forces attacked Sandal Castle near Wakefield in Yorkshire, where York and his second son Edmund were encamped with their army, and defeated the Yorkists, killing both men and later executing the Earl of Salisbury. Their heads were cut off and mounted over the Micklegate Bar, the main entry to the city of York, and the duke's head was adorned with a paper crown, to mock his pretensions to the throne.

Edward was now the heir of York and the throne, and the following February he defeated a large Lancastrian army at Mortimer's Cross in Wales, but the issue was not yet settled. A few days later Warwick's forces, with Henry in tow, were defeated at St. Albans, and the queen again took possession of her husband. Young Richard and his brother George were sent to safety in Burgundy to await the outcome of the struggle. Edward of York was welcomed into London and proclaimed King Edward IV, and on Palm Sunday, March 29, 1461, in an unusually late snowstorm he and his large army defeated the remnants of the Lancastrian army in a bloody battle at Towton. Henry, Margaret, and their son Edward fled into Scotland. The Yorkist age had begun.

When Richard and George returned to England they were created dukes of Gloucester and Clarence, and Richard was sent to Middleham, the stronghold of the Earl of Warwick, to begin his knightly training. It was there that he met Warwick's daughter Anne, and the two became friends. Although Richard was only nine years old, his adored brother Edward bestowed many honors and responsibilities on him, while apparently ignoring George, the elder by three years, and this may have been the beginning of the jealousy that George felt towards both of his brothers for the remainder of his life.

In 1464 Edward IV announced his marriage to Elizabeth Woodville, the widow of a Lancastrian and the mother of two young sons. The two had been married secretly some months earlier, and the announcement caught the court by surprise, causing a rift between the king and Warwick, his greatest supporter and the man most responsible for his success in gaining the crown. The earl had been negotiating for many months for a marriage between Edward and Bona of Savoy, the sister-in-law of the French king, and he never forgave the public humiliation inflicted by the Woodville marriage. He put a good face on it, but the rapid rise of the new queen's large, ambitious family widened the breach, and Warwick began the intrigue which ended in his death and the fall of his branch of the powerful Neville family.

In 1469 Warwick won over, without much difficulty, George of Clarence, who married Isabel Neville, the earl's elder daughter, in a secret ceremony at Calais, but Richard, despite the lure of having Anne for his wife, remained loyal to the king. When Warwick returned to England he was able to capture the king briefly, until he was rescued by Richard and other loyal supporters, without bloodshed. As a reward Richard was named to the powerful positions of Constable of England for life and Chief Justice of North and South Wales.

When Edward learned that Warwick, who continued to instigate rebellions, planned to drive him from the throne and replace him with Clarence, both men were proclaimed traitors and were forced to flee to France. Warwick's anger at Edward and hatred of the Woodvilles were so intense that he joined forces with the exiled Margaret of Anjou in a plan to restore Henry VI to the throne. To seal the pact he married his younger daughter Anne to Margaret's son Edward. Clarence was to succeed to the throne if Edward of Lancaster and Anne had no heirs.

In September 1470, Warwick invaded England and carried out his plan. Edward IV was forced to flee to the protection of his brother-in-law the Duke of Burgundy, where he spent the following months preparing for a return to England to reclaim his crown. In March 1471, he returned, and Clarence, possibly out of a belated sense of loyalty to his family, but more probably out of pique at what he perceived as Warwick's betrayal, deserted his father-in-law and went over to Edward's side. On April 14, 1471, Easter Sunday, the Yorkist king's army defeated the forces of the Earl of Warwick, and he and his brother, the Marquis of Montague, were killed. Richard of Gloucester, then aged nineteen, commanded the right wing of the Yorkist army. By this time, Margaret of Anjou, with her son and his bride Anne in her train, had landed in England, a return delayed by the former queen's insistence that Henry VI should be secure on his throne before she risked the life of her son. Her husband had been captured at Barnet, and the distraught Margaret was all for returning to France, but she allowed her advisors to persuade her to make a stand. The Lancastrians turned toward the Welsh border, intending to join forces with Jasper Tudor and other Welsh supporters, but the Yorkists were close behind, and at Tewkesbury in Gloucestershire they caught up with them. In a fierce battle Edward of Lancaster was killed, crying, according to some chronicles, for succor from his brother-in-law Clarence. The hopes of the Red Rose lay in ruins and Edward returned to London, with the former queen and her daughter-in-law Anne Neville in custody. On that same night, May 21, 1471, Henry VI died in the Tower. The official story was that he died of melancholy upon learning of the death of his son and the capture of his wife, but he was probably killed by order of Edward IV.

Richard was rewarded for his steadfast loyalty by his grateful brother with large grants and powerful positions, including those in the north which had formerly belonged to Warwick. It was at this time that he gained possession of Middleham and Sheriff Hutton, and he was then the greatest of the king's subjects in the north.

The one thing Richard desired above all others was the king's permission to marry Anne Neville, but Clarence, who had gained custody of her, had no desire to share the vast Warwick inheritance. When Richard, having received the king's permission, went to claim his bride, Clarence insisted that she had disappeared, he knew not where. For many weeks Richard and his retainers scoured London, and Anne was finally discovered working as a kitchen maid in the house of one of Clarence's adherents. She was taken to the sanctuary of St. Martin le Grand until the question could be settled.[18]

The quarrel that ensued was public and bitter, with Clarence refusing to give up any of the Warwick inheritance. It was finally settled when Richard declared his willingness to marry Anne without her inheritance, but in the end he was allowed to keep Middleham and other Warwick possessions in Yorkshire, and Clarence kept the remainder of the estate. In the spring of 1472 Anne and Richard were married, and they left immediately for Middleham, where the following year their only child, Edward, was born. After his marriage Richard took under his protection other members of the Neville family who had suffered from the actions of the late earl, including his mother-in-law and Anne's uncle and an aunt.

In 1477, Clarence, who had become increasingly bitter and turbulent, was arrested on charges of treason. Isabel, his wife, had died, and he had expressed his desire to marry Mary of Burgundy, the daughter of the late Charles the Bold. Edward refused to allow the marriage, since it would have greatly enhanced the power of his unstable and envious brother. Clarence reacted with unconsidered fury, accusing two of his late wife's servants of poisoning her, and then executing them, thus infringing on the king's prerogative. He publicly accused the king of planning his destruction, spread the slanderous rumor that Edward was the illegitimate son of the Duchess of York and an archer named Blackburn, and hinted that the king's own children were the spawn of a bigamous marriage. He was tried by the parliament in 1478, with Edward as prosecutor, and the following month was sentenced to death. Richard pleaded in vain for the king to spare his brother's life, and on February 18 Clarence was executed in the Tower. The tale, current both then and now, is that he was drowned in a butt of Malmsey wine, but there is no evidence either to prove or disprove the story.

After Clarence's death Richard left London and returned to Middleham, and it was there that he learned that Edward had died on April 9, 1483. Shortly before his untimely death the king had named Richard Protector and Defender of the Realm of his young son, the future Edward V. Too late he had sought to reconcile the warring factions in his court, the Woodvilles on the one side, and his Chamberlain Lord Hastings and other members of the old nobility on the other. There was a sham reconciliation at the king's deathbed, but as soon as he was dead the infighting to gain control of the new king and the kingdom was resumed.

When his father died, Edward V was in residence at Ludlow, in the care of the queen's brother Anthony, Lord Rivers, and her son by her first marriage, Richard Grey. In an attempt to seize control the queen had called the council and demanded that a large force be sent to bring her son to London for his coronation. Neither she nor the council wrote to inform Richard of his brother's death or his appointment, and she planned to hold the ceremony before her brother-in-law could learn of either. The Woodvilles apparently hoped that by having an immediate coronation there would be no need for a protector, and they could rule through the young king.

These plans were foiled by Lord Hastings, who wrote to Richard, urging him to get to London as quickly as possible, warning him of the danger of delay, both to himself and the realm. Bolstered by the support of the Duke of Buckingham, but with only a small force of men at his back, Richard intercepted the king, Rivers, and Grey at Stony Stratford, arrested the latter two, and accompanied the boy to London. There he learned that another of the queen's brothers, Sir Edward Woodville, aided by her other son by her first marriage, Thomas, Lord Dorset, who was Constable of the Tower, had taken a good part of the royal treasure out of the country, and that the remainder had been divided between the queen and Dorset. These and other equally illegal actions of the Woodville faction finally alarmed those of the council who were loyal only to the king, and a letter from Richard, assuring them of his loyalty to his brother's son, gained him their support.

When the Woodvilles learned of the arrest of Rivers and Grey, and Richard's possession of the king, the queen and her children fled into sanctuary at Westminster Abbey. Preparations continued for the coronation of Edward V, but opposing factions within the council continued to cause problems for the Protector. Buckingham's rapid rise had raised jealousy and resentment in Hastings, Bishop Morton, Lord Stanley, and other members of the late king's party, and Richard learned that they had been meeting secretly and were in communication with the queen, in an apparent attempt to restore the Woodvilles to a position of power.

On June 13, 1483, at a council meeting in the Tower, the Protector accused the conspirators, Elizabeth Woodville, Jane Shore, who was the late king's mistress, Stanley, Morton, Archbishop Rotherham, and Hastings, of treason. Hastings was summarily executed and the others placed under arrest. Morton was sent to Buckingham's castle of Brecon in Wales for confinement. Despite Hastings' popularity among the Londoners, virtually no voice was raised in protest against his execution without trial, but it is probable that many of the citizens believed at this point that Richard planned to take the crown.

The prediction proved true, when a few days later it was announced that, according to Bishop Stillington of Bath and Wells, Edward IV had been contracted in marriage to Dame Eleanor Butler, the daughter of the Earl of Shrewsbury, at the time he married Elizabeth Woodville. Since a contract was, in the eyes of the church, as binding as a marriage, Edward's subsequent marriage was bigamous, and his children illegitimate and so barred from the succession. The truth of this allegation is difficult to establish, but Paul Murray Kendall has suggested that Clarence learned of the contract and lost his life because the queen feared he would disclose it.[19]

Richard was proclaimed the true heir to the throne by Friar Ralph Shaa in a sermon at Paul's Cross on Sunday, June 22. Using as his text "Bastard slips shall not take root," he informed his listeners about the marriage contract. On succeeding days Buckingham addressed the Lords, magistrates and leading citizens, telling them that Richard was the rightful king. On Wednesday, June 25, a de facto parliament met at Westminster, reviewed the charges regarding the late king's marriage, and asked Richard to accept the crown. They presented the petition to him on the following day, and with some reluctance he accepted. He and Anne were crowned in Westminster Abbey on July 6, with virtually every peer and leading citizens of the realm in attendance.

A few weeks after the coronation the king and queen went on progress, travelling around the country to visit and show themselves to the citizens, and when they arrived in Lincoln in early October Richard learned that his friend and supporter Buckingham had rebelled against him. The duke had succumbed to the wiles of his prisoner Bishop Morton, who was deeply involved in a plot of the Woodvilles and Lancastrians to place Edward V back on the throne. When the rumor reached them that the two sons of Edward IV were dead, the plan was changed, and they decided to support Henry Tudor's bid for the crown.* There is little reason to doubt that this was Morton's intention from the beginning.

---

*Dominic Mancini, an Italian who lived in England for several months during this period, wrote that, after Hastings' death, the sons of Edward IV "were withdrawn into the inner apartments of the Tower

In any event, Buckingham's rebellion failed, and he was caught and executed at Salisbury on November 2, 1483. Morton escaped to Flanders to continue his attempts in Tudor's behalf. Tudor himself, waiting with his fleet off Plymouth, returned to France when he learned of Buckingham's death. Some of the conspirators fared better than they could have expected; although a few were executed, the others were pardoned, and Stanley and Northumberland were given many of Buckingham's confiscated estates.

In March 1484, Elizabeth Woodville and her daughters came out of sanctuary, and she wrote to her son Dorset, who had joined Tudor in Brittany, that it was safe for him to return. When he attempted to do so, however, Tudor's agents captured him, and he was forced to remain.

The following month, on April 9, 1484, exactly a year after the death of Edward IV, Richard and Anne's young son Edward died at Middleham, and although the death of the sickly child was not unexpected, his parents never recovered from the tragic loss. The author of the "Second Continuation" of the *Croyland Chronicle** noted that on learning of the death of their son, "in whom all the hopes of the royal succession . . . were centered . . . you might have seen his father and mother in a state almost bordering on madness, by reason of their sudden grief."[20] Anne was at this time already severely ill, probably with tuberculosis, the same disease which had killed her sister Isabel, and on March 11, 1485, she died. As with the death of almost any royal personage of the period, there were rumors that she had been poisoned, and although he was devastated by her death for both political and personal reasons, it was suggested that Richard had hastened her end so that he could marry his niece Elizabeth. Henry Tudor had publicly declared his intention to marry the princess in order to secure the support of the Woodvilles and other adherents of Edward IV, and

---

proper, and day by day began to be seen more rarely behind the bars and windows, till at length they ceased to appear altogether. . . . I have seen many men burst forth into tears and lamentations when mention was made of him [the king] after his removal from men's sight; and already there was suspicion that he had been done away with. Whether, however, he has been done away with, and by what manner of death, I have not at all discovered" (The Usurpation of Richard III, translated by C.A.J. Armstrong; London, 1969, page 93). Although Mancini was a conscientious reporter, he knew no English and was unacquainted with English customs. He made serious errors in dating several events, including Edward IV's death, and omitted the dates of others, such as Hastings' death. Nevertheless his account is valuable because it preserves current rumor about the fate of the princes and others events.
**The Continuator is generally believed to have been John Russell, Bishop of Lincoln, a member of Edward IV's Council and Richard III's Chancellor.*

some people may have believed that Richard intended to marry her to circumvent Henry's plans. The king, however, publicly denied any such intention and blamed the rumors on Tudor and his supporters.

In August, Henry Tudor, with an army composed of French mercenaries and led by his uncle Jasper Tudor and the Earl of Oxford, landed in Milford Haven in Wales. Tudor, who had never in his life fought in a battle, marched under the standard of the red dragon of Cadwallader, claiming descent from that ancient Welsh king. He marched through Wales with little opposition, gaining support, thanks in part to promises of lavish rewards to all who would join him, and on August 22, 1485, he met the king's army on Redmore Plain outside the town of Market Bosworth in Leicestershire. Tudor's army numbered probably five thousand men, including the two thousand Frenchmen. The king's army was roughly twice that size, but the forces of the Stanleys, Henry Tudor's stepfather and his brother, were of uncertain loyalty, as were the three thousand men under the command of the Duke of Northumberland, Richard's rival for control of the north. The Stanleys were obviously going to wait to see how the battle went before they committed their forces, thus ensuring that they would come in on the winning side. Northumberland refused to engage his men at all, and sat out the battle on the sidelines.

When the king realized that his only hope for survival depended on killing Tudor, he and several of his loyal supporters made for the standard of the red dragon, behind which Henry waited, protected by his experienced commanders. As the king was about to reach the pretender, having struck down his standard-bearer, the Stanleys entered the battle on Tudor's side, and Richard was doomed. Crying "Treason! Treason!" he was struck down and hacked to death, and after the battle, according to the often-told tale, his crown was recovered from under a bramble bush by Sir William Stanley, who placed it on Henry Tudor's head, to cries of "Long Live King Henry!" The naked, bloody body of the late king, with a felon's halter around his neck, was thrown across his horse, which one of his heralds was forced to ride, and taken to Leicester. His battered body was taken to the church of the Grey Friars, where it lay for three days, exposed to all eyes, until the friars received permission from the new king to bury it in an unmarked grave, without ceremony. Some years later, the penurious Henry VII allotted the sum of ten pounds one shilling for a tomb for his predecessor, but during the reign of Henry VIII, and the dissolution of the monasteries, the simple tomb was destroyed, and the bones of the last Plantagenet were thrown into the Soar.

Henry Tudor dated the beginning of his reign from the day before the battle, so that he could brand as traitors and fine all who had fought against him. His claim to the throne was tenuous, at best, since he was descended from two illegitimate lines, neither of which had any legal right in the succession. On his father's side he was descended from the union of Katherine of Valois, the widow of Henry V, and Owen Tudor, a minor Welsh squire; there is some question about whether the two were legally married. Tudor's mother, Margaret Beaufort, was the daughter of John, Duke of Somerset, the grandson of John of Gaunt and his third wife, Katherine Swynford. Since the children of this union were born before their parents' marriage, they were barred from the succession by an act of Richard II's parliament.

In order to secure his title it was necessary for the new king to put forth every argument that legitimized it. It was for this reason that he had promised to marry Elizabeth of York, the eldest daughter of Edward IV, a promise which brought him the support of many disaffected Yorkists. It was obvious that Henry did not relish a marriage to the daughter of his hated enemy, the man who had forced him into a life of exile and penury, and he was long in carrying it out. Elizabeth was not crowned until after the birth of her first child, and a good deal of pressure from her supporters.

The most significant step toward creating a climate of acceptance of his rule, and the one with the most long-lasting effects, was the systematic blackening of his predecessor's name. Several of the early histories written in Henry's reign, by historians in his employ, contain the beginnings of the legend of the monstrous Richard so familiar today. John Rous, a cleric and historian who had written flatteringly about Richard III during his lifetime, discovered, when he was no longer king, that he had lain two years in his mother's womb, been born with teeth, long hair, talons, and a hump, and had murdered Henry VI, his nephews, and his wife Anne. Bernard André, the tutor of Henry's son Arthur, added other murderous traits to Rous' characterization, and portrayed Henry Tudor as the saintly, noble leader sent by God to deliver England from Richard's clutches. This theme was taken up by most of the later Tudor chroniclers from whom Shakespeare got his material.

Polydore Vergil, who appears in Anderson's play as one of the main inventors of the Tudor version of history, was an Italian cleric who came to England in 1502, and in 1507, at Tudor's request, began his *Anglica Historia*, which covered English history from the earliest times until 1509. One modern writer referred to Vergil as "a paid liar,"[21] which is certainly too harsh a judgment, but even Speed, one of the Tudor chroniclers, declared that he is "not to be rashly beleeved."[22] Vergil's *Historia*, noted Antonia Gransden, was an apologia for the House of Tudor, and "was intended to spread Tudor propaganda by means of the scholars whom it persuaded."[23] It is perhaps understating the fact to say that it succeeded beyond the most optimistic hopes of its creators.

The man usually given the most credit, or blame, for the creation of the Tudor myth is Sir Thomas More, whose *History of King Richard the Third*, considered the first English history of any literary merit, was printed first in Grafton's *Chronicle*, and then in those of Hall and Holinshed, the major sources of Shakespeare's history plays. More, who lived for a time in the household of Bishop Morton, doubtless learned what he knew about Richard from that politically astute churchman, and there are indeed some who believe that Morton was the actual author of the *History*. This is probably wishful thinking, an attempt to remove what they consider a black mark from the character of a man in other respects so worthy of admiration.

More incorporated much of Rous' description of Richard's origins, appearance, and character, and made some colorful additions of his own. He described the king as "little of stature, croke-backed, his left sholder much higher then his right, hard-favored of visage.... He was malicious, wrathful, envious..." and he had a withered, shrivelled arm.[24] More added the suggestion that Richard murdered Henry VI without his brother's knowledge, and may have murdered Clarence as well.[25] This possibility became a certainty in later histories and fiction.

The notion that a deformed body and an ugly face are the outward manifestations of an evil mind and wicked heart is, of course, not confined to any age or culture. Cinderella was good, therefore she was beautiful; her stepsisters were wicked, therefore ugly. In the land of Oz the wicked witch was ugly, the good witch beautiful. Richard III was evil, therefore he was ugly and deformed; Henry Tudor's angelic appearance was confirmation of his noble heart and mind.

Maxwell Anderson employed the same principle in *Richard and Anne*, only his ugly villain and handsome hero are not More's or Shakespeare's. In the stage directions Anderson, using the well-known portrait as his guide, describes Richard as having "a handsome face, somewhat stern and sad, and a slight but vigorous frame." Henry Tudor, on the other hand, is depicted as a rat-like creature who, when cornered, clicks his teeth and scurries to and fro, and his character in this play is very much in keeping with his appearance. Anderson's contempt for Henry is evident in an earlier play as well. In *Anne of the Thousand Days*, when Anne Boleyn asks Henry VIII about large amounts of money he has acquired, probably illegally, he tells her:

> I am the son of Henry the Seventh. I studied under a real master — my father. Whatever crookedness was lacking in the world when my father was born he invented before he left it. No other king of our island ever stole so widely, so successfully, so secretly — or died so rich.

When Anne asks him if his father killed for money, Henry replies, "It was his main source of income — to attaint a well-lined noble for treason, do away with him, and take what he had. It brought in millions."

The martyrdom of Jane Shore, the kindhearted "merry mistress" first of Edward IV and then of Lord Hastings and the Marquess of Dorset, by the cruel Richard, was another of More's inventions, and one that has given rise to numerous romantic poems and novels. It was More who disclosed the story of the marriage contract between Edward IV and Eleanor Butler, except that he gave her name as Elizabeth Lucy, who was one of that monarch's many mistresses.

It was More's version of the murder of the princes in the Tower, however, that has stamped Richard III as the irredeemable villain so brilliantly portrayed by Shakespeare. Although More admitted that he had heard many different stories about the fate of the boys, and that many people had doubts about whether they had in fact been murdered, he believed the one he gave to be the truth. Most people since that time have believed it as well. Edward V and his brother Richard were, according to this version, smothered in their beds by agents of their uncle, and then buried at the foot of a stairway in the Tower. When the king learned about their burial place, he decided it was not a fitting grave for royal princes, and so the bodies were removed to some unknown place. During renovations to the Tower in the reign of Charles II some bones were discovered under a stair-well and proclaimed to be the remains of the sons of Edward IV, murdered on orders of their uncle; they were placed in an urn in Westminster Abbey.

This tale might well have faded into memory, like that of King John murdering his nephew Arthur so that he could claim the throne, or those of other ambitious and not too scrupulous monarchs, had it not been for the genius of Shakespeare, whose memorable play has imprinted on our memories the portrait of ultimate evil. It does not matter that the character of Richard is almost a caricature, and that the plays in which Richard appears, *Henry VI, Parts II and III*, and *The Tragedy of King Richard III* contain many anachronisms and errors of fact. They are great drama, and most people care not at all that they are not historically accurate. The Duke of Wellington is said to have remarked that he never read history, and the only history he knew he learned from Shakespeare. Shakespeare has, in fact, created our vision of the history of the period.

While the reputation of Richard III, who was held in generally high esteem during his lifetime, has suffered since his death, that of Henry VII has fared well only by comparison. The Tudor chroniclers who painted Richard in such dark colors portrayed Henry as an angel sent by God to deliver England from the cruel usurper. Hall describes Henry as "a man of no great stature, but so formed and decorated with all gyftes and lyniamentes of nature that he seemed more an angelical creature than a terrestriall personage."[26] Polydore Vergil, who of course knew Henry and admired him greatly, describes him as remarkably attractive, noting that "his eyes were small and blue, his teeth few, poor and blackish; his hair was thin and white; his complexion sallow."[27] Vergil praised Henry not only for his fine appearance, but for his firmness, his kindness to all who would submit to him, and his undoubted abilities as an administrator and tax-gatherer.

It was not until the early Stuart period that a writer of any note offered a somewhat balanced view of the first Tudor monarch. In 1621, in disgrace and exile in his country home of Gorhambury, Sir Francis Bacon began to write *The History of the Reign of King Henry the Seventh*, partly to pass the time, and in part, perhaps, in an attempt to regain the favor of James I by portraying his ancestor as a man with a genius for government. Whatever his intentions, it is Bacon's portrait of Henry VII as a capable, indeed brilliant, monarch, but a mean, grasping, secretive tyrant, which has come down to us. Bacon was, of course, much harsher to Richard, and accepted all of the charges against him, but he criticized Henry on several counts: first that he had delayed his marriage to Elizabeth of York so that none should think that he owed his title to her; that he had deprived Elizabeth Woodville of all her possessions and shut her up in a nunnery "without any legal proceeding, upon far fetched pretences that she had delivered her two daughters out of sanctuary to King Richard, contrary to promise"; that his agents extorted money from people; and that he executed Clarence's son on a trumped-up charge of treason.[28]

For the first four hundred or so years after his death in 1485 the historical Richard III was not the controversial figure he is today. Until the nineteenth century few people questioned the truth of Shakespeare's portrayal of the cruel tyrant, the deformed murderer who destroyed his brother, nephews, Henry VI and his son Edward, his own wife, and others who stood in his path to the throne. Although there were a few writers who came to his defense before that time, none wrote during the Tudor period, when praise of Richard III, or indeed any of the Plantagenets other than Elizabeth of York, wife of Henry VII, was actively discouraged.

The earliest serious defense of Richard III, *The History of the Life and Reigne of Richard III*, was written in 1619 by Sir George Buck, one of whose ancestors had been executed after the Battle of Bosworth for fighting on the losing side. Although the work, which was not published until 1646, many years after Buck's death, contains many errors, it was the first attempt to show that the sources upon which the so-called "Tudor Myth" are based were prejudiced and unreliable.

Nearly a hundred and fifty years passed before another author came to Richard's defence. In 1768 Horace Walpole published *Historic Doubts on the Life and Reign of King Richard the Third*, and although this work, like Buck's, contained some errors, its influence was, and continues to be, substantial. Walpole attacked the sources on which the character of Richard III rested, as Buck did before him, and expressed the belief that the princes in the Tower were not murdered. According to Walpole, Perkin Warbeck, the pretender who invaded England with the support of the Duchess of Burgundy, Richard's sister, and the kings of Scotland and France, claiming to be the younger of the two princes, was in fact the son of Edward IV, and furthermore, he wrote, Henry VII's reaction to Warbeck shows that he believed it too.

These early attacks on the sources of the Tudor version of the life and reign of Richard III did not bring about any sudden conversion in the vast majority who believed that Shakespeare's and More's version were true, but they began a dialogue which continues to this day.

Beginning in the nineteenth century, a few works of history and fiction appeared in which Richard III was portrayed in a more sympathetic light, but these works did little to improve his image. In 1951, however, mystery writer Josephine Tey wrote what has become the most widely read and influential defense of Richard III. In *The Daughter of Time* she dissects the Tudor Myth and skewers its inventors, saving her harshest words for Thomas More. Richard emerges as an almost saintly figure, and is proved innocent of all the crimes laid at his door. Richard III now has many defenders, not a few influenced by Tey, and thousands of them worldwide have joined together in the Richard III Society, an organization formed to educate the public about his life and times.

A veritable flood of pro–Richard novels followed the publication of *The Daughter of Time*, and although there are still novelists who prefer Shakespeare's more traditional, and interesting, monarch, they are, at present, vastly outnumbered. Maxwell Anderson's *Richard and Anne* fits very well into this revisionist pattern, and it is of incomparably greater merit than most of the works in the genre.

Although few people have seen or read *Richard and Anne*, its existence has been known to members of the Richard III Society and others for many years. On August 19, 1955, Sam Zolotow reported in *The New York Times* that

> everything has been hush hush regarding Maxwell Anderson's theme in the forthcoming play. Although it could not be verified from official sources yesterday, it was learned that the central character is Richard III. Instead of depicting him as the bloody king of popular conception, he emerges in the untitled script as a maligned hero.

Zolotow noted further that I. Stanley Kahn, a member of the New York Stock Exchange, had spent three years doing research about Richard in the British Museum and elsewhere in England and had turned over his findings to Anderson. The Playwrights' Company and Mr. Kahn were to produce the resulting play. The stockbroker had announced the previous March that he planned to put on a dramatization of Josephine Tey's *The Daughter of Time*, and would put "the wealth of material on the historical doubts" about Richard III at the disposal of whomever wrote the adaptation.

Inspired by Tey's *The Daughter of Time*, Anderson had begun writing *Richard and Anne*, originally titled *A Shadow and a King*, in January 1955, intending to have it produced by the Playwrights' Company. Although he was one of the founding members, the company turned down *Richard and Anne*, and in a letter to the members of the company dated April 1956, he announced his intention of resigning for the reason that the disadvantages to playwrights of membership far outweighed the advantages. He noted that it had become a general producing company, rather than an organization of playwrights, and was producing plays which members did not choose, finance, or control, and often did not like, while member playwrights, who did not have the option of offering their works to any producer except the Playwrights' Company, were made to feel that any of their plays which had been turned down were not worth producing, "which is not always true."

In his disappointment at having not only *Richard and Anne* but his 1953 play *Devil's Hornpipe*, turned down, Anderson suggested that the Playwrights' Company, although it had produced some great plays, was not suited to being a producer, and that the production end should be put into business hands, and the playwrights be given the freedom to offer their works to other producers.[29]

Anderson's disappointment at the rejection of *Richard and Anne* was probably mixed with surprise, since a friend and fellow-writer whose opinion he respected had read the play and praised it enthusiastically. In a letter dated August 29, 1955, Robert Sherwood noted that his "serious criticisms are solely concerned with the framework — the trimmings of the play rather than the play itself."[30] He offered several suggestions, but compared this work very favorably with *Joan of Lorraine*,[31] concluding, "I feel mighty happy about your new play and don't see why you shouldn't plan for production as soon as you can get a director and leading actors."[32]

Apparently Anderson did not try to interest another producer in *Richard and Anne*, since no further mention is made of it in his letters. The script of the first draft, handwritten on some seventy legal-size sheets, including revisions, is now with the author's other papers in the Harry Ransom Humanities Research Center at the University of Texas at Austin. Anderson revised and expanded the play, taking into account some of Sherwood's suggestions, adding new scenes and characters, but maintaining the basic form and content.

The McFarland edition is the play's first publication, and there are only three documented readings of either version of the play. The first was on October 3, 1981, at the Annual General Meeting of the Richard III Society, held at the Explorers Club in New York City. With the permission of Mrs. Maxwell Anderson, a member of the Society, and Anderson's literary executors Brandt and Brandt, a reading of *Richard and Anne* was given by Stefan Rudnicki, a playwright and the chairman of the Theater and Film department of C.W. Post College, with professional actors and members of the college theater company.

About a year after the New York reading, the play was put on in Stamford, Connecticut, the first production of what is now the Maxwell Anderson Playwrights Series. This series, which is produced by Mrs. Maxwell Anderson, presents staged readings of previously unproduced, unpublished plays, some of which have gone on to professional production. In addition, the company produces one Maxwell Anderson play each year. On October 10 and 11, 1992, a series of three readings of *Richard and Anne* marked the tenth anniversary of the Maxwell Anderson Playwrights Series in the Greenwich Arts Center in Greenwich, Connecticut.

Anderson wrote plays with both contemporary and historical settings, ranging from ancient Greece (*Barefoot in Athens*), to early America (*Valley Forge* and *Knickerbocker Holiday*), and his interest in English history is evident in some of his best known plays. These include *Elizabeth the Queen*, *Mary of Scotland*, and *Anne of the Thousand Days*, sometimes referred to as the Tudor Trilogy. Anderson did his own research for the historical background for all his plays, but the inaccuracies to be found in many of them can be attributed to poetic license rather than lack of knowledge. There are in *Richard and Anne*, as in Anderson's other history plays, some inaccuracies and anachronisms, but generally he sticks fairly close to the known facts.

Maxwell Anderson occasionally repeated certain dramatic devices, and in *Richard and Anne* we see evidence of three from his earlier plays. In *Joan of Lorraine* we have a play within a play, in which the actors portraying historical characters are affected or influenced by the characters they play, as are the writer and director of the show. *Richard and Anne*, however, can be said to have two plays within a play, one of them Shakespeare's *Richard III*, and the other the true story of Richard and Anne, who influence to some extent both the actors portraying them on the stage and others involved in the production.

The device of having contemporary characters interacting with long-dead historical or imaginary characters was used very effectively in *High Tor*, one of Maxwell Anderson's best plays, and later with equal effect in *Richard and Anne*. In *High Tor*, a verse play written and produced in 1936 and published in January 1937, all of the characters are imaginary, whereas in *Richard and Anne* the contemporary characters and one of the ghosts are fictional, and Richard and the rest of his contemporaries in the play are, of course, historical.

Dag, the jester in *Richard and Anne*, is able to move backward and forward through time, but his purpose is not to change things as they actually were, but only to change the reputation of his beloved master, whose true character has been so perverted by writers since his time. (In *The Star Wagon*, 1937, the inventor hero uses his time machine to go back and try to change the past. He discovers, however, that the changes he is able to make do not improve his life or those of his loved ones, since the wealth and power he acquires corrupt him and destroy his soul. He chooses, therefore, to return to his old life, for he realizes that although he has failed to achieve financial success, his life has not been a failure.) When Richard asks Dag to let him change his past, he tells him it cannot be done. Richard cries, "Who wants his life again if it's to be unchanged? Who wants it the way it was?" The one thing he wants to change above all is Anne's dying belief that he loved someone else. If he can let her know the truth, that he never loved anyone but her, he will go back to his grave content. By calling up people from his past, and showing how things really were, Dag, and then Richard, hope to change the world's perception of him as well, but his disappointment when he realizes that this is not possible is philosophic rather than bitter. The words and the vision of a great poet seem more real than the truth he and Dag have revealed to the audience, and he accepts it. His mission, if not Dag's, has been accomplished, and he can return to his resting place. Shakespeare's *Richard III* will be performed the following night.

Few people will dispute the notion that history is written by the winners, or that the few voices raised in defense of the losers tend to be dismissed as irrelevant. Anderson raised this point in an earlier play, *Mary of Scotland*, in which the Scottish queen tells Elizabeth that, although she was now triumphant, she, Mary, will win in the end when the histories are written. Elizabeth replies:

> It's not what happens
> That matters, no, not even what happens that's true,
> But what men believe to have happened. They will believe
> The worst of you, the best of me, and that
> Will be true of you and me. I have seen to this.
> What will be said about us in after-years
> By men to come, I control that, being who I am.

In 1954 Anderson returned to the theme of a monarch's attempt to control both the course of history and his or her future reputation. In *Masque of Queens*, an unpublished two-act play, he shows Queen Elizabeth at the end of her life attempting to prevent the succession of Mary's son James by supporting the candidacy of a young earl who reminds her of Essex.[33] She was, of course, unsuccessful, and James VI of Scotland became James I of England after her death in 1603.

Richard, like many of the heroes in Anderson's tragedies, was a victim both of circumstances over which he had no control, and of flaws in his own character. He was unable to control the jealous factions in his court, and his willingness to trust people like the Stanleys, and in this play Henry Tudor and Morton, even after they had proved themselves unworthy, was almost suicidal. Even when he returns from the grave he is almost an innocent in his lack of suspicion, and he has to be convinced that not only has his reputation been destroyed, but that Henry Tudor was responsible.

Anderson's treatment of Richard and Anne, and his harsh indictment of Henry Tudor, Bishop Morton, and Stanley, are to be expected in a work of a writer whose aim was to counteract the propaganda of the Tudor writers. Somewhat surprising, however, is his rather sympathetic treatment of Elizabeth Woodville, whom most defenders of Richard III view as a greedy, manipulative schemer, and certainly no friend of her late husband's family. Anderson's view of the queen, however, has great dramatic impact as it underscores the villainy of Richard's enemies, and helps to explain her willingness to trust him by sending her daughter to live at his court.

Maxwell Anderson greatly admired rebels, men and women who would not take orders from those in authority. Brom, the hero of *Knickerbocker Holiday*, declares, "I can't take orders. No matter how hard I try, I simply cannot take orders from anybody." In *Elizabeth the Queen* Essex loses his life because he will not, or cannot, take orders, even from the queen. Of course, in his case, it was his desire to take her throne and thus be in a position to give the orders that caused his downfall, but Anderson saw him as a strong and independent hero who refused to sacrifice his integrity for expedience, even at the cost of his life. The rebel in *Richard and Anne* is not Richard, but the jester Dag. There is, of course, no need for him to obey the orders of the stage manager or director since he is able to control what goes on on the stage, and can escape them simply by vanishing. But he defies Richard, his beloved lord, as well. Dag makes up the rules of the game, and it will be played by his rules or not at all. He wants only to tell the truth about Richard, and thus restore his reputation, and he attempts to thwart Richard's attempts to tell Anne of his love. When Richard realizes that Dag is in love with Anne and jealous of her love for Richard, he challenges him, and Dag reluctantly agrees to try to help him.

The ending of *Richard and Anne*, as in so many of Anderson's plays, is pessimistic but not hopeless; Shakespeare's *Richard III* will indeed be performed on the next and many nights to come, and although many people will continue to think of it as historical truth, there will always be some who will challenge the accepted version. In time, perhaps, though they may not prevail, they will make a difference. For Maxwell Anderson, the romantic realist, the lover of lost causes, this may have been enough.

Notes to the Introduction

1. "Anderson Memoir," a thirty-four page transcript of a May 10, 1956, interview with Maxwell Anderson conducted by Louis M. Starr in the Oral History Collection at Columbia University. Laurence G. Avery, *Dramatist in America: Letters of Maxwell Anderson, 1912–1958* (Chapel Hill: University of North Carolina Press, 1977), 308–309.

2. John Mason Brown, *Two on the Aisle* (New York: W.W. Norton, 1938), 208–209.

3. Alfred S. Shivers, *Maxwell Anderson* (Boston: Twayne Publishers, 1976), 96–97.

4. Maxwell Anderson, Preface to *Knickerbocker Holiday* (Washington, D.C.: Anderson House, 1938), v.

5. *Ibid.*, vi.

6. Shivers, *Maxwell Anderson*, 92.

7. Avery, *Letters of Maxwell Anderson*, 241–242. Laurence G. Avery, compiler, *A Catalogue of the Maxwell Anderson Collection at the University of Texas* (Austin: Humanities Research Center/University of Texas at Austin, 1968), 75, 139.

8. *Fanfare* (September/October, 1992), 391.

9. Avery, *Letters of Maxwell Anderson*, 29–30.

10. Maxwell Anderson, "Poetry in the Theater," *Off Broadway* (New York: William Sloane, 1947), 50.

11. "Anderson Memoir," 315–316.

12. John Gassner, *Masters of the Drama*, 3rd rev. and enl. ed. (New York: Dover Publications, 1954), 678–680.

13. Maxwell Anderson, "Off-Broadway," *Off-Broadway*, 28.

14. Obituary, *The New York Times*, March 1, 1959, 84.

15. "Anderson Memoir," 307.

16. Obituary, *The New York Times*, 84.

17. Maxwell Anderson, "The Essence of Tragedy," *Off-Broadway*, 58–59.

18. *Ingulph's Chronicle of the Abbey of Croyland*, translated by Henry T. Riley (London: Henry G. Bohn, 1854), 469–470.

19. Paul Murray Kendall, *Richard the Third* (New York: W.W. Norton, 1956), 147.

20. *Croyland Chronicle*, 496–497.

21. Philip Lindsay, *The Tragic King: Richard III* (New York: Robert M. McBride, 1943), 233.

22. John Speed, *The History of Great Britaine*, 3rd ed. (London: G. Humble, 1632), 723.

23. Antonia Gransden, *Historical Writing in England, II, c. 1307 to the Early Sixteenth Century* (Ithaca, N.Y.: Cornell University Press, 1982), 439.

24. Sir Thomas More, *The History of King Richard the Third*, vol. II of *The Complete Works of St. Thomas More*, ed. by Richard S. Sylvester (New Haven, Conn.: Yale University Press, 1963), 7–8, 48.

25. *Ibid.*, 8.

26. Edward Hall, *Chronicle* (London: J. Johnson; F.C. and J. Rivington, et al., 1809), 416.

27. Polydore Vergil, *Anglica Historia*, ed. by Denys Hay, vol. 74 of *Camden Third Series* (London: Royal Historical Society, 1950), 145–147.

28. Sir Francis Bacon, *The History of the Reign of King Henry the Seventh*, ed. by Roger Lockyer (London: Folio Society, 1971), 46, 53–56, 207–209.

29. Avery, *Letters of Maxwell Anderson*, 278–279.

30. Letter to Maxwell Anderson in the possession of Mrs. Maxwell Anderson, p. 1.

31. *Ibid.*, p. 3.

32. *Ibid.*, p. 4.

33. Avery, *Catalogue of Maxwell Anderson Collection*, 73–74.

Two Letters
(Robert Sherwood)

25 Sutton Place   August 29th, 1955
New York 22, N.Y.

Dear Max,

Vic sent me "Richard and Anne" to the hospital — from which I have just, somewhat shakily, come home — and I am happy to be able to render a good report. I was amazed at how strongly and effectively the main Richard story comes through — the amazement being due to grave doubts I had held (when I heard in a general way what you were attempting) that you might be biting off more than you or anyone else could chew. But I thought your story soared above its framework and the final concession of victory to the Poet is a superbly moving resolution.

My serious criticisms are solely concerned with the framework — the trimmings of the play rather than the play itself. I don't know what you must do about this, but it must be imaginative work rather than mere carpentry. You have made the management — Kent, Leger, etc. — so literal and earthy that when the riot squad is sent for, one expects the riot squad to arrive momentarily. Al, the stage manager, on the other hand, seems to have a wonderful sense of the fact that something is going on that takes this theatre out of space, out of time. As I said, I am helpless to offer any suggestions — but it is possible you might make a bit more use of the traffic cop (Accard) who considers the theatre as a crazy place, anyhow, and not always controllable by the rules and regulations of the Police Dept., or by any conceivable

law, or even by any conceivable Max Gordon or Laurence Langner
or whomever. I suspect that Accard and Al should see, or sense, that
it won't do Kent any good to call out the riot squad, or the entire U.S.
Marine Corps: if wraiths and spirits choose to invade a theatre, who
is to stop them? for it is the only natural habitat they have left on
earth — the only remaining House of Wonder. I feel there must be a
moment when we see Kent admit defeat, possibly early in the second
act; he is baffled & bewildered & even scared, & knows he has no
recourse but to retreat to a bar across the street. He might even tell
the audience to get their money back at the box office.

I think, but am not sure, that you may be in danger of overdo-
ing the farcical opportunities early in the play. It would be a great
mistake to have Dag represented or even suggested as a pixieish
leprechaun whose appearances & vanishings are merely impish mis-
chief. He is a desperately sad clown who is seriously demanding a
hearing. I don't like the idea that the real Richard story must fight its
way out of a paper bag of irrelevant comedy, and then continue with
the fear that this paper bag may be re-imposed by the playwright at
any moment.

I doubt that I have made myself at all clear. If I have, it must be
delusive, because I am by no means clear in my own mind what I am
trying to say. But I am quite clear what I want to see, which is that
the fine substance of your play be untrammeled by attendant, subor-
dinate shadows. I am certain that you can accomplish much more in
this one than you did even in "Joan of Lorraine."

My only possible criticism of the unfolding of the main story
comes in the Anne-Richard scene around page 2-16. Here, for a moment or so, Richard seemed to be almost like a business-man husband
explaining to the little woman why he must take off for a swing around
the Middle West, rather than the tragic victim of the Tudor poison
which is already beginning to destroy happiness and life itself for him
and Anne. This is only a matter of a speech or two which may be
misleading. The one real problem, in my opinion, is in the framework, and I beg that you will seek to solve that by poetic and imaginative rather than by practical means. One thing that you will never
have to make this play is "logical" — and thank God for that!

I am going away to the country (not far) for ten days or so, but
I guess I won't be functioning normally for some time.

In the meantime, I feel mighty happy about your new play and don't see why you shouldn't plan for production as soon as you can get a director & leading actors. (N.B. — I don't think the same actress should play the Player Queen & Anne, although you seem to suggest this in a stage direction on page 1-34.)

Yours,
Bob

("Richard and Anne")

I-12-19 — Much too much of Shakespeare.

25-31 — Too much Accard. It seems to me straining it to have Accard exerting so much effort to trip two unwanted actors. There's much more comedic value in his preoccupation with his own job — the traffic — and, besides, his horse is waiting for him.

31-32 — Kent and the riot squad still seem wrong to me, and I'm sure it's a mistake for him to name a span of time, 15 minutes, when the wraiths may have the stage to themselves.

August 30, 1955

Dear Max:

Yesterday I wrote you about your play and sent the letter to the
Playwrights' office. Vic tells me that he has sent it on to you in Beverly
Hills. Last night Madeline read the play. I had not told her one word
about it or given any indication of my opinions, but she vehemently
agreed with my enthusiasm for it and with the feeling that you must
do something to make the framework less literal; and she expressed
confidence that you would accomplish this easily because it is inherent
in the whole strange spirit of the play. She said that the manager,
director, etc., should simply be bewitched — and added that she was
bewitched merely reading it. When Kent reappears near the end and
seeks to do the last scenes of "Richard III," Dag and Richard have
largely had their hearing and the bewitchment is naturally wearing
off.

Both Madeline and I feel that the curtains of both acts are wonderfully
good and that there is no need to try to tamper with either one. You
may remember that Madeline loved JOAN OF LORRAINE when
she first read it. Well, she loves RICHARD AND ANNE even more
and feels sure that it will be completely clear and convincing to the audience.

When I wrote you yesterday I neglected to thank you for the hearten-
ing note that you sent me when I was in the hospital.

Yours,
Bob

Cast of Characters
in order of appearance

Al, the stage manager
Gates, the Player King, the actor portraying Shakespeare's Richard III
Dag, Richard III's jester
Charlie, the assistant stage manager
Stage hand, a voice offstage
Leger, the director
Kent, the producer
Player Queen, portraying Anne Neville in Shakespeare's *Richard III*
Four noblemen, serving as pallbearers
Richard III
Officer Joseph Accard, a policeman
Clarence, the brother of Richard III and Edward IV
Isabel Neville, Anne's sister and Clarence's wife
Anne Neville, wife of Richard III
Henry Tudor
Archbishop Morton, advisor to Henry Tudor
Clink, the butler in Clarence's London home
1st girl, a servant in Clarence's London home
2nd girl, a servant in Clarence's London home
Man-at-arms
Bishop Stillington
Prince Edward, son of Richard III and Anne Neville
Edward IV
Elizabeth Woodville
2 children of Edward IV
2 servants
Julius Caesar
William the Conqueror

Lord Rivers
Lord Hastings
Lord Stanley
Lord Grey
Herald
3 ladies-in-waiting to Elizabeth Woodville
Alison, companion to Anne Neville
Elizabeth of York, daughter of Edward IV
Several nobles and ladies
Polydore Vergil
3 or 4 policemen

Act One

*The lights go up on the curtain and there is a
premonitory trembling along its surface as if it were
about to rise. However, it settles back and a man's
voice is heard backstage, calling somewhat peremp-
torily.*

Voice   Places please! Did you hear me? I said places
please! Curtain going up!

Second Voice   *(Also a man's, backstage.)* I heard you! Is he supposed to be on stage?

First Voice   I said places! I'll have to take the curtain up the
way we are if you — !

Second Voice   Take it up then! Damn that fool! I can't —

First Voice   Damn what fool?

Second Voice   That fool! That jester, there! Can't you see him?

First Voice   No, I can't! And for the last time, places! Curtain going up! I mean it!

Second Voice   Then get that jester off stage!

First Voice   Quiet!

Second Voice   Get that — !

First Voice   Quiet!

*(The curtain rises, revealing the Player King alone on
the stage in the costume of Richard III and against a
background of black curtains. His was the second of the
two voices. He now faces the audience and somewhat*

	shakily begins to speak the opening soliloquy of Shake- *speare's Richard the Third.)*
PLAYER KING	Now is the winter of our discontent Made glorious summer by this sun of York And all the clouds that lowered upon our house In the deep bosom of the ocean buried. *(While the Player King speaks a jester of the time of* *Richard III begins to appear against the curtains in the* *background. He is seated on a low stool, cap in hand,* *and his eyes are fixed on the Player King, who does not* *see the jester but seems to feel his gaze.)* Grim-visaged war hath smoothed his wrinkled front, And now, instead of mounting — *(The Player King pauses, The stage manager, whose* *voice was first heard, prompts him.)*
STAGE MANAGER	"—instead of mounting barbed steeds —"
PLAYER KING	—instead of mounting barbed steeds — *(But instead of continuing the Player King turns, as if* *against his will, and looks at the jester.)* To fright the souls of fearful adversaries, He — *(He pauses.)*
STAGE MANAGER	"He capers nimbly in a lady's chamber —"
PLAYER KING	He — capers —
STAGE MANAGER	"Nimbly —"
PLAYER KING	Nimbly — in a lady's chamber — *(He pauses, in agony, unable to recall.)*
STAGE MANAGER	"To the lascivious pleasing of a lute."
PLAYER KING	I can't — I can't think of the words and I can't say them While he sits there saying the words are wrong —

	The words are wrong —
STAGE MANAGER	"To the lascivious pleasing — "
PLAYER KING	Damn it!

PLAYER KING (continued):

Damn it, will you take this clown away
Where I can't see him? Is there supposed to be
A clown in Richard III? He wasn't there
When I studied the part, but he's there now, and he drives me
Half insane, mouthing and — Will you get him away
Before I forget where I am? *(To the audience.)* I'm sorry — I'm —
I'm truly sorry — forgive me.

STAGE MANAGER *(Appearing.)* Shall I ring down the curtain?

PLAYER KING Get him away!

Get him offstage and — Damn him, why does this happen?
Why does this happen now?
(To the audience.) I'm sorry. Forgive me.

STAGE MANAGER What clown do you mean? Where is he?

PLAYER KING There! Sitting there!

STAGE MANAGER *(Seeing the jester for the first time.)* What? Who are you? Clear the stage please. Come.

(He turns to the audience.)

Ladies and gentlemen, I'm sorry about
This interruption. We'll resume in a moment.
Keep your seats, if you will, and — I apologize
To you and to the cast. Some stranger seems
To have wandered on stage out of a costume party
And thrown us into confusion. Come with me, sir.

(To the clown.) You've
Come in the wrong door, my boy, so step this
way —
This way, if you please.
*(The jester sits still, looking steadily at the stage
manager who begins to be impatient, and goes forward
as if to lay hands on the intruder. He pauses, however,
for the stage is illuminated as if by a flash of summer
lightening, and the jester is now not to be seen.)*
He must have slipped through the curtains!
(To his assistant offstage.)
See if you can find him, Charlie, and put him
outside!
(To the audience.) If you'll forgive us we'll take
the curtain down. And start all over. I'm sorry
about this, sir.

PLAYER KING   He's still here.

STAGE MANAGER   Who?

PLAYER KING   The clown.

STAGE MANAGER   I don't see him, sir.

PLAYER KING   I don't either. He comes and goes. He'll be here
When I start to speak.

STAGE MANAGER   We'll get rid of him
And try again. Charlie, ring down the curtain.

CHARLIE   *(Offstage.)* I've been trying to, Al. Something's
wrong.

STAGE MANAGER   And what happened to the lights? Was that a
fuse that blew?

CHARLIE   Not back here.

A VOICE   *(Offstage.)* The lines are tangled.

STAGE MANAGER   When did this happen?

THE VOICE   *(Offstage.)* Just now. It worked at rehearsal.

STAGE MANAGER	*(To the audience.)*
	I'm sorry. When things go wrong everything goes wrong.
	Forgive us another minute.
	(He walks off into the wings.)
PLAYER KING	*(Looking out at the audience.)*
	Is Mr. Leger out there?
A VOICE	*(From the audience.)*
	He's coming back, Mr. Gates. He'll be right with you.
PLAYER KING	Ladies and gentlemen, I'm not out of my mind,
	But I get half way through a speech, and that jester appears,
	Sitting somewhere on the stage, and my mind goes blank,
	And I—
	(Mr. Leger, the director, comes on stage.)
	Mr. Leger, nobody can believe this,
	But I try to speak, and every time that jester
	Appears, somewhere on stage, and I can't think.—
	This is Mr. Leger, ladies and gentlemen,
	Who directed the play, and here's Mr. Kent, the producer.
	(Mr. Kent enters from the wings.)
	And I'm sorry to let them down.
	(Mr. Kent and Mr. Leger bow to the audience.)
KENT	Forgive us both for being here on the stage. I'd rather be out front myself, and so would Mr. Leger, I think, but we're in a rather peculiar jam. The play's stopped and the

curtain won't come down, so something has to be done and I guess we have to do it. Joe, will you take over?

LEGER   You see, Mr. Gates, Mr. Kent and I were out front together, and it seemed to us there was only one thing to do. We had an uninvited guest at our party, but he's gone now and the natural thing is to forget the whole episode and start from the top.

PLAYER KING   Again?

LEGER   You're a bit shaken, Mr. Gates, and of course it's the usual thing to take the curtain down when you have to start fresh. It just happens that there's a mechanical failure and we don't have that little springboard—and since we don't have it—well, we'll have to make ourselves jump in without it. We'll leave the stage, the stage manager will say "Curtain" and off you go.

PLAYER KING   You'll leave the stage, but he won't.

KENT   Who won't?

PLAYER KING   Whoever that is! *(He points to the spot where the jester was seen before, and there he is as we first saw him.)*

LEGER   Al!

STAGE MANAGER   *(Entering.)* Yes, sir.

KENT   Get this joker out of the theater!

STAGE MANAGER   I'll do my best, Mr. Leger, but every time I try to lay a hand on him he evaporates.

KENT   Nonsense! Nobody evaporates! You sir! We want to use this stage and you're in the

	way! Outside, please! *(The jester doesn't move.)*
Leger	Al!
Stage Manager	Yes, sir.
Leger	Put him on the street.
Kent	We don't like to be rough, you know, But if necessary we will be. *(The jester continues to regard them steadily, with unblinking eyes.)* All right, Al. *(To the jester.)* There are three of us to your one. *(Kent, Leger and the stage manager advance on the jester. There is a flash of light again and the jester is gone.)* What kind of conjuring trick is this?
Stage Manager	It's the way I told you, Mr. Kent. When you try to touch him, he's not there.
Kent	At any rate he's gone now.
Player King	But if I say three words of my part he'll take center stage again.
Leger	Try it.
Player King	*(Taking his place for the soliloquy.)* Well— "He capers nimbly in a ladies chamber To the lascivious-pleasing—" *(The jester has appeared again. The Player King stumbles and stops.)* I can't go on. The words are gone from my mind.
Kent	Who are you? How do you come here? *(A pause.)*
The Jester	I come a long way. You should have known my master. There was a man accustomed to command.

                    You do it cheaply.
LEGER   Why do you dress yourself in this ridiculous
                         costume and interfere with the presenta-
                         tion of this play?
THE JESTER   I've wondered myself.
                    It may be that when venom is poured over
                         bones
                    For centuries, and the lies touch someone you
                         love,
                    It reaches the quick at last and you stir in your
                         grave,
                    And can't lie quiet, and get up and walk—
                    And search—and find out this evil—where it
                         lives—
                    And try to fight back.
KENT   What evil?
THE JESTER   Deliberate, poisonous, vicious calumny
                    Of those I loved, of my good lord and mistress,
                    Slander of their love, as pure as the love
                    Of children—for it was the love of children—
                    They were cousins and grew up together, loving
                    Even then.
KENT   You say we have slandered your master—
                    Who was your master? We slander no one!
THE JESTER   Richard!
                    The Richard you cartoon with the lump on his
                         back,
                    And the withered arm—making love to some-
                         body's widow!
                    After he killed her husband, and killed his
                         father!
LEGER   Are you speaking of Richard the Third?

                Richard died in 1485 —
                Could hardly have been your master.
THE JESTER   I was the fool.
                I was the fool they kept at Middleham
                To sing at supper. I loved my lady. She died
                Of grief when her son died. Four months later
                      my lord
                Was killed at Bosworth, and pushed into a
                      grave
                Without rites, near Leicester. I lived on under
                      Henry,
                The peddler king.
KENT   But this is ridiculous!
THE JESTER   There was no marker on Richard's grave,
                But I marked it, and had myself buried there
                Under that same drip of serpents' tongues
                That drenched my master's bones.
                Well, after a certain number of centuries
                Of that bitter drink, the grey bones gather to-
                      gether
                In desperation, and a whirl of dust comes round
                      them,
                And once again anger and love stare from the
                      eyes.
                For I loved my mistress and my lord. It is —
                It is ridiculous, and forlorn, and hopeless!
                But I come to stop that wash of scurrilous stuff
                With these broken hands. To stop it at the
                      source —
                Here where it's made. So when he stands before
                      me,
                Your player king, he cannot say the lines,

	Because they're lies.
KENT	You came to stop *Richard Third?*
THE JESTER	I came to stop *Richard Third.* And I have
	stopped it.
KENT	It's been played ten thousand times! Did you
	allow
	The first ten thousand?
THE JESTER	Sir, it may be
	That the first ten thousand are the easiest.
	I never did understand our human life,
	And our human death's no simpler. That septic
	drip
	Grew less bearable with the centuries.
	Grew unbearable in the end—and here I am.
KENT	It has to be
	On opening night?
THE JESTER	It chances to be
	On your opening night. And there will be
	No Richard Third such as you've always
	known,
	With crooked back and black smile and dull knife
	And Tower full of dead children!
LEGER	There's no other Richard!
THE JESTER	I knew another.
	His bones washed down with mine to that little
	scurf
	Of trash at the bottom of the field. I had
	No trouble telling his occiput from the one
	I used to wear. His was the king's. Mine had
	The cap and bells still on it—gone dirt color
	And partially dissolved. *(He indicates his head-*
	gear.)

	But he was a king!
	If I could rouse him and bring him here you
	would see
	Another kind of Richard!
KENT	*(Winking at Leger.)* Yes, I believe it, but you see
	our problem's
	To put a play on here tonight. We've promised
	Richard Third, and rehearsed it. The audience
	Paid to get in, and it's not fair to give them
	Nothing because you think there's something
	wrong
	With the Richard story. It's been given so often
	How could one more time matter?
LEGER	And see, they're waiting.
KENT	They've been very patient.
LEGER	Could you police
	Every English-speaking stage, to the end of
	time.
	To keep them from giving this play?
THE JESTER	No.
KENT	And even if it's not given
	Why wouldn't it be read? And if it's read
	What have you gained?
THE JESTER	Nothing. Yes, I've gained nothing.
	(He bows his head in his hands.)
KENT	After tonight
	Come in and put your hex on us if you like,
	But let us go on now.
LEGER	Just for this opening
	Let us follow the program that was promised.
	After that—well, we'll take our chances.
KENT	What do you say? Will you give us

This one night? *(They pause and wait. The jester*
       doesn't answer verbally but he begins to fade
       and soon is only a wraith before them.)
The answer's yes! Yes, ladies and gentlemen,
He begins to fade before us, as you see,
And we can start in a moment!

LEGER   Mr. Gates,
       Is Rosalind ready?

PLAYER KING   Yes, all made up and waiting.

LEGER   Good! Now, I'll tell you —
       If the audience doesn't mind, and Mr. Kent
       Says yes — we've lost so much time, let's not go back
       To the top,
       But start with the second scene,
       And pick up from there.

KENT   It's all right with me.

LEGER   And with you, Hal?

PLAYER KING   Yes, by all means. *(He sees that the jester has quite*
       vanished.)
       Let's get on with it. *(He goes out.)*

LEGER   Al!

STAGE MANAGER   *(Offstage.)* Yes, sir?

LEGER   Don't bother with the curtain! Twelve!

STAGE MANAGER   *(Offstage.)* Right. Places!
       Places for twelve!

LEGER   We'll get off.

KENT   Yes. *(Kent and Leger go out. The lights come up.*
       The stage is empty, and music is heard, a
       funeral march with oboes. Four noblemen enter,
       carrying a coffin on their shoulders. The Player
       Queen follows them in mourning. The Player
       King enters, meeting them.)

PLAYER KING	Stay, you that bear the corse, and set it down!
PLAYER QUEEN	What black magician conjures up this fiend?
PLAYER KING	Villains, set down the corse!
PLAYER QUEEN	What, do you tremble? Are you afraid?

(The nobles set down the coffin and retire.)

	Avaunt, thou dreadful minister of hell!
PLAYER KING	Sweet saint, for charity, be not so curst.
PLAYER QUEEN	Fool devil, for God's sake, leave and trouble us not!
PLAYER KING	Lady, you know no rules of charity!
PLAYER QUEEN	Villain, thou knowest no law of God nor man.
	No beast so fierce but knows some touch of pity.
PLAYER KING	But I know none and therefore am no beast.
PLAYER QUEEN	Oh, wonderful, when devils tell the truth!
PLAYER KING	More wonderful, when angels are so angry.
	I did not kill your husband.
PLAYER QUEEN	In thy foul throat thou liest! Queen Margaret saw
	Thy murderous falchion smoking in his blood!
PLAYER KING	I was provoked by his slanderous tongue.
PLAYER QUEEN	Thou wast provoked by thy bloody mind!
	Didst thou not kill this king?
PLAYER KING	I grant ye.
PLAYER QUEEN	Dost grant me, hedgehog? Then God grant me, too,
	Thou mayst be damned for that wicked deed!
	He is in heaven, where thou shalt never come!
PLAYER KING	Let him thank me that holp to send him thither,
	For he was fitter for that place than earth.
PLAYER QUEEN	And thou unfit for any place but hell!
PLAYER KING	Yes, one place else, if you will hear me name it.

PLAYER QUEEN   Some dungeon.

PLAYER KING   Your bed-chamber.

PLAYER QUEEN   Ill rest betide the chamber where thou liest!

PLAYER KING   So will it madam till I lie with you.

PLAYER QUEEN   I hope so.

PLAYER KING   I know so. *(During the next ten lines the jester begins to appear, this time not seated but standing to the left of the group that includes the Player King and Queen. And when he is fully embodied the wraith of another figure begins to form beside him. It is the Richard III we see in the portraits, with a handsome face, somewhat stern and sad, and a slight but vigorous frame. He and the jester are absorbed in the scene that is playing.)*

But, gentle Lady Anne,
Is not the causer of the timeless deaths
Of these Plantagenets, Henry and Edward,
As blameful as the executioner?

PLAYER QUEEN   Thou art the cause!

PLAYER KING   Your beauty was the cause!
Your beauty, which did haunt me in my sleep
To undertake the death of all the world
So I might live one hour in your sweet bosom.

PLAYER QUEEN   If I thought that, I tell thee, homicide,
These nails should rend that beauty from my cheeks!

PLAYER KING   You should not blemish it if I stood by.
As all the world is cheered by the sun
So I by that. It is my day, my life.

PLAYER QUEEN   Black night o'ershade thy day, and death thy life!

PLAYER KING	Curse not thyself, fair creature—thou art both.
	It is a quarrel most unnatural
	To be revenged on him that loveth you!
PLAYER QUEEN	It is a quarrel just and reasonable.
	To be revenged on him that slew my husband!
	(A pause.)
PLAYER KING	I've lost my words. That jester's here again, Al.
STAGE MANAGER	*(Prompting.)* "He lives that loves thee—"
PLAYER KING	He lives that loves thee better than he could.
PLAYER QUEEN	Name him.
PLAYER KING	Plantagenet.
PLAYER QUEEN	Why that was he.
PLAYER KING	The self-same name, but one of better nature.
PLAYER QUEEN	Where is he?
PLAYER KING	Here. *(She spits.)* Why dost thou spit at me?
PLAYER QUEEN	Would it were mortal poison, for thy sake!
PLAYER KING	*(Aside.)* Damn!
STAGE MANAGER	"Never came poison—"
PLAYER KING	Never came poison from so sweet a place!
PLAYER QUEEN	Never hung poison on so foul a toad!
	(A pause.)
PLAYER KING	Look, Al, he's back again, and he's brought a friend.
	I just can't think with these extras around.
STAGE MANAGER	*(Prompting.)* "Teach not thy lips—"
PLAYER KING	Teach not thy lips such scorn, for they were made
	For kissing, lady, not for such contempt.
	(A pause.) Damn!
RICHARD	We're in the way here, Dag. This gentleman
	Resents our presence.
THE JESTER	This is your queen and you.

RICHARD   Let us not be unmannerly. I think

We're less noticeable here. *(He draws the jester to the left.)*

THE JESTER   But this is your queen —

Your queen and you.

RICHARD   Where?

THE JESTER   The Player King

Is you, my lord, and the Player Queen's your queen,

The Lady Anne, my mistress.

RICHARD   There's no likeness.

THE JESTER   But this is how you are known.

RICHARD   With a lump on my back?

THE JESTER   And a belly full of murders,

Hateful to your own lady.

RICHARD   Silent, and listen.

Proceed, gentlemen.

PLAYER KING   We have your permission?

RICHARD   Kindly proceed.

STAGE MANAGER   "Lo here —"

PLAYER KING   Lo, here I lend thee this sharp-pointed sword

Which if thou please to hide in this true bosom

And let the soul forth that adoreth thee,

I lay it naked to the deadly stroke,

And humbly beg the death upon my knee.

(He kneels and bares his bosom.)

Nay, do not pause, for I did kill King Henry,

But 'twas thy beauty that provoked me.

Nay, now dispatch — 'twas I that stabbed young Edward,

But 'twas thy heavenly face that set me on.

(She drops the sword.)

	Take up the sword again, or take up me.
PLAYER QUEEN	Arise, dissembler. Though I wish thy death,
	I will not be the executioner.
PLAYER KING	Then bid me kill myself, and I will do it.
PLAYER QUEEN	I have already.
PLAYER KING	Tush, that was in thy rage.
	Speak it again, and even with the word,
	That hand which for thy love did kill thy love
	Shall for thy love kill a far truer love.
PLAYER QUEEN	I would I knew thy heart.
PLAYER KING	'Tis figured in my tongue.
PLAYER QUEEN	I fear me both are false.
PLAYER KING	Then never man was true.
PLAYER QUEEN	Well, well, put up your sword.
PLAYER KING	Say then my peace is made.
PLAYER QUEEN	That you shall know hereafter.
PLAYER KING	But shall I live in hope?
PLAYER QUEEN	All men, I hope, live so.
PLAYER KING	Vouchsafe to wear this ring.

(He offers a ring. She hesitates, then holds out her hand.)

PLAYER QUEEN	To take is not to give.

(He places the ring on her finger.)

PLAYER KING	And if thy poor devoted suppliant may
	But beg one favor at thy gracious hand?
PLAYER QUEEN	What is it?
PLAYER KING	That it would please thee leave these sad de-
	signs
	And presently repair to Crosby place,
	Where, after I have solemnly interred
	This noble king,
	And wet his grave with my repentant tears,

<table>
<tr><td></td><td>I will with all expedient duty see you.
Grant me this boon.</td></tr>
<tr><td>PLAYER QUEEN</td><td>With all my heart, and much it joys me too
To see you are become so penitent.</td></tr>
<tr><td>PLAYER KING</td><td>Bid me farewell.</td></tr>
<tr><td>PLAYER QUEEN</td><td>'Tis more than you deserve. (She hesitates again,
then lets him kiss her, and goes out.)</td></tr>
<tr><td>PLAYER KING</td><td>Was ever woman in this humor wooed?
Was ever woman in this humor won?
I'll have her, but I will not keep her long.
What! I, that killed her husband and his father,
To take her in her heart's extremest hate,
With curses in her mouth, tears in her eyes,
The bleeding witness of her hatred by,
And I nothing to back my suit at all
But the plain devil and dissembling looks,
And yet to win her, all the world to nothing!
Ha!
Hath she forgot already that brave prince
      whom I
Stabbed in my angry mood at Tewkesbury?
And will she yet debase her eyes on me,
On me that halt and am unshapen thus?
Upon my life, she finds,
My self to be a marvellous proper man!
I'll entertain a score or two of tailors
To study fashions to adorn my body!
Shine out, fair sun, till I have bought a glass,
That I may see my shadow as I pass!
(He capers a little, watching his shadow. There is
some scattered clapping at the rear of the audience.
Richard, obviously amused, smiles at the Player King</td></tr>
</table>

	and claps with the others, not over-enthusiastic, not too patronizing. The four nobles pick up the corpse and carry it out.)
DAG	Master!
RICHARD	Yes, Dag? *(The Player King bows and goes out.)*
DAG	Can you applaud this?
RICHARD	Very deft and amusing.
DAG	This is the sulphuric leech that's eaten Its way down through the rubble there at Leicester And bitten into your good years, yours and my lady's, Till my earth felt the sting, and came to hear it— And roused you too.
RICHARD	Well, it's a tale of a king Who murdered and smiled his way to what he wanted, And it's done so cleverly it's like a jewel, Every facet perfect.
DAG	But this is you!
RICHARD	Well, the name's Richard. There have been many Richards, One like this perhaps. Not I.
DAG	It's told About you and your lady.
RICHARD	Then perhaps This is one version of what we were like.
DAG	This is the only version—and in all histories This is the way you're known.
RICHARD	It's not possible.
DAG	It's the way you're known to men. In these times about us

                        This is what men think of you.
RICHARD   But who would have
                        An interest in writing lies?
DAG   Why, your successor
                        Henry Tudor.
RICHARD   And why should lies be told?
                        What end would it serve? No, Dag, we should
                            have slept
                        And let them amuse themselves. *(He draws Dag
                            further toward stage left.)*
KENT   *(Shouting from the rear of the auditorium.)*
                        Al! Al! Are we going to have a curtain?
AL   *(Emerging from the wings.)*
                        Yes, Mr. Kent?
KENT   *(Shouting.)* Don't we get a curtain?
AL   It's not working yet, Mr. Kent! We've been
                            trying it!
LEGER   *(From the rear of the auditorium.)*
                        Then we'll have to go on without it! Straight
                            into thirteen!
AL   Right. *(He goes offstage.)* Places, please. Thirteen.
PLAYER KING   *(Appearing stage right.)*
                        Mr. Leger?
LEGER   *(Still in the auditorium.)* Yes? *(Player Queen comes on
                            in background.)*
PLAYER KING   It's all very well to say we'll go ahead with thir-
                            teen, but you saw what happened in this
                            last one! Those two standing around,
                            and I go up every time I see them — or
                            think about them!
PLAYER QUEEN   I don't think I can say my lines, Mr. Leger!
                            Not with —

LEGER	We have to do the best we can! We have to give as good a performance as possible!
PLAYER QUEEN	Is Mr. Kent there?
KENT	*(Coming on stage from right.)* I'm here. We'll put an end to this now! *(He stalks directly across the stage, breathless and angry.)* I want you two offstage! Both of you! And I want you to stay off!
RICHARD	We were about to go, sir.
KENT	You said that before, and you came back! You annoy the actors and the audience! This is a theatre and we try to give satisfaction to the customers! You're making the whole thing impossible! Now when you get offstage this time, I want it to be final. I want you to stay offstage!
RICHARD	We shall not annoy you further, sir.
KENT	*(To the jester.)* That goes for you, too! You haven't said anything, and you're the one that started it! You're the one I don't trust! *(Leger enters and follows across toward Kent.)*
DAG	You're most flattering.
KENT	Do you mean that you intend to go out and stay out, or do you intend to return the way you did before?
DAG	Sir, do you consider yourself the injured party?
KENT	If I'm not the injured party I don't know who is! When I put a play on I feel responsible to the actors and the people in the audience and the investors! They've all got an interest in seeing this show done well! What right have you to climb onto

     our stage, get in the way of the performers, spoil the audience's fun, throw the actors out of work, and ruin the investment?

DAG   What right have you to say of my king that he was a liar and a murderer?

KENT   Now, come, we know that can't be true! You can't be the king or his fool, or any of that! You may belong to some society that's set out on a Carrie Nation binge to right the wrongs done the last Plantagenet! I've heard of that group of displaced paranoids! If that's your game play it in some theatre where they can afford it! We're just trying to put on *Richard Third!*

DAG   That's the play you cannot perform! That one!

LEGER   But why? *(The Player King and Queen slip offstage quietly.)*

DAG   There must come an end to the lies!

KENT   I've heard enough of that, too! Who says it's lies? Richard the Third of England was the biggest liar, murderer, thief, brigand, and hypocrite that ever sat on any throne anywhere! He killed, he murdered, he betrayed, he double-crossed every man, woman and child that got in his way! He married any woman that had something he wanted, and wrung her neck when he was through with her! Everybody knows this! It's in all the histories! You can't rewrite English history! This play doesn't say anything the histories don't say!

RICHARD	Dag, I'm sorry. It seems to be true.
DAG	It is true.
KENT	So clear out and let us alone! Get off the stage! And now, or I'll find someone to lock you up! *(To the audience.)* I beg your pardon for blowing up, ladies and gentlemen, but this sort of behavior is beyond belief! A man comes to the end of his patience! *(To Dag and Richard.)* Now, can we have the stage?
RICHARD	Sir, have you read a great deal of history?
KENT	Some other time —
RICHARD	I must know this now.
KENT	Listen, old-timer, I never went to school much, I don't know much history, but one king everybody knows is Richard Third! He was a double-tongued, two faced butcher, as crooked inside as out! Does that satisfy you? Can we end this?
RICHARD	*(To Dag.)* This is the story they know.
DAG	Yes, master.
KENT	Will you clear the stage?
DAG	Not for this play!
KENT	Al!
AL	*(Entering.)* Yes, Mr. Kent?
KENT	There's an officer on duty outside the theatre. Ask him to step in for a minute.
AL	Yes, sir. *(He goes out. Kent comes briskly downstage and looks up.)*
KENT	Can we do anything with that curtain?
LEGER	Al sent a man up, but he says we'll need a ladder on stage.

(They look at the curtain above them.)

KENT   We'll let it go then. We'll have to.

LEGER   I want to say a word to the actors.

KENT   Right. *(Leger goes out.)*

RICHARD   *(To Kent.)* You seem to be in some authority here. —
I know, sir, that all causes fail in the end;
That all our lives are tragic, for all men die;
That nothing will be settled in our time —
Nor in any time. But this I did not know,
That the truth would not sometime out. I had
            presumed
That as the years went on and the evidence
Was sifted by new generations, all we were
Would be seen, would be known.

KENT   *(Humoring him.)* That's right, murder will out.

RICHARD   But will the truth out? The plain tale
Of Richard and Anne is this: When he was
            fourteen
He went to live with his uncle Warwick. His
            playmates
Were Warwick's daughters, Isabel and Anne.
Anne was eleven. Richard's brother, George,
Chose Isabel, Richard loved little Anne.
When Richard was nineteen and Anne sixteen
They were married. This gay, mocking brilliant
            scene
You played here,
With a crippled king who has killed a lady's
            husband
And the husband's father,
And now makes love to the lady, yes, and wins
            her,

Wins her brutally, over the father's corpse,
What has this to do with Richard or my Anne?
I did not kill the husband nor the father;
Nor had she been married. We were in love
And had been many years.

KENT   *(To the audience.)* We'll clear this up in a moment,
                  ladies and gentlemen. By the way, I
                  don't want to be discourteous to any-
                  body, but at this point I find myself with
                  rather little to say to those two lunatics
                  at my left. Meanwhile I want to thank
                  you for being extraordinarily patient.
                  I've been in on a lot of plays, and I
                  thought I'd seen everything, but I never
                  went through anything like this!

AL   *(Looking in.)* Mr. Kent?

KENT   Yes?

AL   The officer's here.

KENT   Good. Ask him to come on stage. *(Officer Joseph
                  Accard comes in, dressed for mounted traffic
                  duty.)*

ACCARD   On stage?

AL   Yes, sir.

KENT   We're having a little difficulty here, Joe —

ACCARD   Yes, Mr. Kent?

KENT   These two strangers rambled in off the street
                  and they keep interrupting our play —

ACCARD   Disturbing the peace?

KENT   You could certainly call it that. I'd like to see
                  'em run in. And now.

ACCARD   These two?

KENT   Those two.

ACCARD   They're in costume.

KENT   They came that way. I think they belong to some group that's opposed to putting on *Richard Third,* so they walked in here deliberately to make trouble.

ACCARD   *(Uneasily, looking out at the audience.)* I never had to do this before. Interrupting the performance, eh?

KENT   Yes.

ACCARD   *(Stepping further on stage.)* Come on boys. No more horse-play. Out the stage door. *(Dag and Richard don't move.)* You heard me, I think. You told 'em to get offstage?

KENT   More than once.

ACCARD   Come on boys. Don't make extra trouble for me, because that'll mean extra trouble for you. Your place is on the street. Step outside. *(Dag and Richard are still immobile.)* I don't want to make confusion here, Mr. Kent, but if they won't come along I'll have to—

KENT   Go ahead.

ACCARD   So far, it's only a misdemeanor, boys, but if it goes any further it'll be resisting an officer, and that's serious. *(He steps toward Dag and Richard.)* O.K., if you want it that way. Out the stage door! On the street! *(There is a flash of light, and Dag disappears. He turns toward Richard, who also vanishes.)* What kind of hocus-pocus is this? Hey?

KENT   I'm blessed if I know, Joe. They pulled that on me, too.

ACCARD   Oh, they did? Have they got any paraphernalia
              with them? You know, Houdini stuff—
              boxes and lay-out?

KENT   I didn't see any.

ACCARD   What's your stage manager's name?

KENT   Al.

ACCARD   Hey, Al, watch the wings there.

AL   *(Coming in.)* Yes, sir.

ACCARD   You watch the stage door. Mr. Kent will watch
              in front.

              I'll go back of these curtains.

              (Dag reappears in his path.)

DAG   I should warn you, sir, that if you step too near
              me—if you step, let us say, beyond this
              line of light—you will forget who you are
              and why you came here.

ACCARD   What kind of game is this now?

DAG   It's not a game, sir.

ACCARD   It's tricks, then.

DAG   No, not tricks. But come near me, come be-
              yond this line, and you will forget who
              you are and why you came.

ACCARD   *(To Kent.)* What's playing in this theatre?

KENT   We're putting on *Richard Third.*

ACCARD   I saw a hypnotism routine once in vaudeville.
              This isn't that kind of thing?

KENT   I don't know what these fellows are up to. We're
              playing Shakespeare.

ACCARD   And you want them out of here?

KENT   We certainly do.

ACCARD   He certainly looks like he was dressed for your
              show.

Kent	There's no fool in *Richard Third*.
Accard	It's Shakespeare, isn't it?
Kent	Yes, but no fools in this one.
Accard	No? Well, how do you tell which ones have fools and which ones don't? Same difference to me. *(To Dag.)* All right, I won't cross your line, but move, now! Move! *(Dag is still motionless.)* You don't leave me any choice, do you? — Look, I don't want to arrest you. My motto is, never start a commotion if you can settle matters amicably. So come on, let's settle it without attracting attention.
Dag	I tried that.
Accard	You're not trying it now.
Dag	No.
Accard	What are you trying?
Dag	I'm seeking for justice.
Accard	You're liable to get justice if you're not careful, and maybe more than you want of it. *(To Al.)* Watch that door now.
Al	Yes, sir. *(He goes out stage right.)*
Accard	*(To Kent.)* You'll watch this side?
Kent	I'll stay right here.
Accard	Because when a guy draws a line and dares me to step across it I step across it, and put the arm on him. *(He goes purposefully toward Dag, crossing the line of light that falls between them. Dag doesn't move. There is again a glimmer of lightning, succeeded this time by a distant rumble of thunder that begins*

far away and seems to come closer—ending in a violent clap. Accard puts his hand to his forehead and stops.)

DAG Have you forgotten something, sir?

(There is a pause while the officer tries to think.)

KENT What's the matter?

ACCARD Damned if I know. *(He reaches instinctively for his revolver. A sandbag falls from the flies and hits the stage about three feet to his right. Another lands about three feet to his left. Kent catches the officer's arm and pulls him downstage.)*

ACCARD What are you doing? *(A sandbag hits where the officer was standing.)*

KENT They were dropping sandbags around you. *Leger reenters.)*

ACCARD Just a minute! Are you one of these or one of them?

LEGER What do you mean by them?

ACCARD Them in there! *(He catches Leger's arm.)*

LEGER Aren't you a little confused?

ACCARD I sure am.

KENT Mr. Leger is our director.

ACCARD Sorry. *(He drops Leger's arm.)*

KENT That's the fellow I want you to do something about. *(He points to Dag.)*

ACCARD I don't want to be made a spectacle of! Did you bring me in here to hypnotize me?

KENT I brought you in to make an arrest!

ACCARD That would be very funny. A cop reaching for a guy and suddenly he goes nuts in front of the audience!

KENT You know me, Joe! I'm putting on a play! This isn't a review!

ACCARD   How do I know what's what here? There's an actor, and he's on stage in costume, and you want me to arrest him. You all look like the same bunch to me. You better come down to the station house and bring formal charges.

KENT   But we can't go on with the play till we get rid of them!

(Al comes in from stage right.)

ACCARD   I can't spend the night on this, you know! I've got traffic outside and it's probably jammed all the way across town by now!

LEGER   I don't think you ought to leave it this way, officer!

ACCARD   One thing I know—I'm not stepping across his lines again—that I do know! *(He goes out stage right.)*

KENT   Well, I don't take that for an answer, audience! We'll go a little higher up in the police department. We'll put this play on if we have to call out the riot squad! Right, Mr. Leger?

LEGER   The actors are standing by. They're game.

KENT   I've got a couple of friends at headquarters. *(He starts off.)*

LEGER   You're going to call them?

KENT   I am.

LEGER   What happens till then?

KENT   Till—? *(He pauses.)* Well, *(To Dag.)* You've got about fifteen minutes to tell your version! See if you can hold an audience with it! Ladies and gentlemen, maybe these historical pranksters can amuse you while I get the police to help us! Any of you who don't want to watch their charades can step out and get a drink. Hang on, everybody, and I'll make my calls! *(He pulls a little book from his pocket and consults it as he goes off. Leger and Al turn to follow.)*

LEGER You know, I'm not sure it's going to do any good to call the police department.

AL Something pretty peculiar happened to Joe.

LEGER Something very peculiar. *(They look at Dag, who has kept his place, and go out. Dag rises and opens a fold of the curtain behind him. Richard comes in.)*

RICHARD You begin to frighten me, Dagonet. What have you done? What power do you have?

DAG Master, I don't know.
Lying there in the earth, I tried to rise,
And I did rise. There was such a burning in me
I couldn't rest. The fire bit still at my vitals,
So I called you, and you came. When we were
    here
I looked at the ropes and tried to tangle them —
And they were tangled. Then this officer,
I made a tangle in his mind. Some power
I seem to have, even now.

RICHARD Whose dream are we dreaming?

DAG I don't know that.
It may be the dream of the spirit world.
It may be yours — or mine.

RICHARD What's next to do?

DAG My king, I brought you here to speak.

RICHARD   But, Dag,
             This is your project, your affair.

DAG   No. You were the king.
             It was you they injured.

RICHARD   *(To the audience.)* When he's alive a king com-
                     mands, but when
             He's dead, his fool commands him. Long ago,
             When Anne and I were young, this fellow sang
             For us and for the guests, in the winter eve-
                     nings
             At Middleham. He was said to be
             A descendant of Merlin. He could call spirits up
             And make them appear. I never knew quite
                     how.
             I don't know now how I'm here — nor any of
                     this,
             This prestidigitation, shall we say —
             That brings me from my grave and lets me see
                     you,
             And you see me. It's some kind of science
                     mixed
             With miracle, like the rest of life, I suppose.
             Mystery and miracle. I lay under weeds at the
                     bottom
             Of a plowed land. I was content to sleep there,
             For the lies were old and no longer hurt, but he
                     came
             And called me, and I'm here.

DAG   These are the living
             Who believe the lies. I was not content.
             I writhed in my grave under that virulent rain,
             And writhed awake, and woke you.

RICHARD	What can I say?
	Say that I was maligned—and make my bow—
	And back to fertilize rag-weed?
DAG	We must play it out.
RICHARD	Play it out in scenes—extempore—?
DAG	As it was.
RICHARD	I'm here alone.
DAG	I'll call them back.
	You shall have anyone you like.
RICHARD	Even Anne?
DAG	Even Anne. But when you see her,
	If you speak to her, you must never say
	A word that would let her know it's not the first time
	The word was spoken, or she'll go back to dust
	When she knows this.
RICHARD	You want me to say only
	The words said long ago?
DAG	If you can remember,
	As near as you can remember.
RICHARD	Who can recall—*(To the audience.)*—
	Who of you can—can recall the words,
	The aimless, spider-web words you said in one hour
	To your lady, or the words she said, or the way
	She turned and spoke? Every man's past is like
	A night in summer, lit by one dim-wit fire-fly,
	Flashing unpredictably on the darkness,
	Lighting a face speaking a half-phrase, then
	Silence, blank, dark, maybe a glimmer again
	A little further on. From these glimmerings
	Can I weave the threads of a day, bring back the words,

The way we stood and moved? It would not be
    true—
It would be all lies if I fudged such a scene,
Pretending that it occurred.

DAG   But let me bring her.
And she will remember a little.

RICHARD   Yes, perhaps,
She would remember some words, and I some
    words,
And she some moods and glimpses, and I some,
But when we put them together we'd have only
Something meditated, written out fair,
    made-up,
Something that never happened. Old times are
    like
Last year's grass in winter. It won't go back.
You can't put it back green again.

DAG   *(Whispering.)* Have I come all this way
For nothing?

RICHARD   Yes, Dag, for nothing, save for one thing:
To see Anne I would play any game, for these
    or for any,
For you if you like. And, boy, this is true of
    you, too.
You loved my lady.

DAG   I—

RICHARD   Have we come all this way,
Both of us, to see Anne?

DAG   Are you angry, master?

RICHARD   *(Smiling.)* We have shared a grave
For a number of centuries. No.

DAG   What day shall we live?

RICHARD   Am I to choose?

DAG   Yes, master.

RICHARD   Then let it be
             The day we met first after she was grown,
             And I'd forgotten her.

DAG   It was at Middleham,
             And I was with you. We had ridden there
             After the battle in which her father died.
             This was the hall. *(A trace of stone-work appears on
                  the curtain.)*
             Clarence had entered. *(Clarence is seen, armed.)*
             This *(A girl's figure emerges from the shadow)*
             Is Isabel. You followed Clarence in.
             And I came after. *(Richard rises and enters the
                  scene. Dag follows him.)*
             Sitting behind her sister,
             And rising slowly to greet us — for she's been
                  weeping —
             Is Anne. Whom you'd forgotten. *(But no figure
                  appears behind Isabel. They wait a moment.
                  Richard looks back at Dag.)*

RICHARD   *(Whispering.)* But she's not here.

DAG   *(Whispering.)* Let me call her again. She was
                  weary of her life.
             She lies in the chancel with your son and hers
             And doesn't wish to rise. Anne, Lady Anne!
                  (They wait a moment.)
             Will you call her, my lord?

RICHARD   *(Whispering.)* Anne! Lady Anne! *(After a pause the
                  figure of Anne, looking much like the Player
                  Queen, but dressed youthfully, appears seated
                  behind Isabel, a kerchief at her eyes. She*

becomes aware of the men who have entered and
rises, drying the tears hastily.)

CLARENCE   Isabel! Wife Isabel!

ISABEL   Clarence! Can I ever trust you again?

              My father is dead! You betrayed him, fought
                  against him!

CLARENCE   Treason is not treason when it succeeds.

              Loyalty is treason when it fails.

              Your father failed.

ISABEL   I hate you!

CLARENCE   Come, kiss me, wife.

              I am your husband. You will not hate me long.

              Come—we shall see to that. *(They go out together*
                  to stage left.)

RICHARD   Forgive me, lady.

              But Warwick's younger daughter, my playmate
                  once,

              Is she not here? Her name was Anne.

ANNE   My name is Anne.

RICHARD   She was a child.

              We played in the fields together.

ANNE   It may be she's grown

              And become a woman.

RICHARD   You know her? She is here?

ANNE   I am Anne.

RICHARD   I believe you are.

              I am Richard. You called me Dickon.

ANNE   Oh, I knew you.—You fought in these wars.
                  You were

              A leader of armies.—I'd be proud of you, only

              My father died in the battle. You could have
                  saved him.

RICHARD

No.

He fought in another part of the field. — Let me

see you. —

Anne — I've thought of you. —

I come back and find you, and your face

Is still the face I love.

ANNE

You didn't know me.

RICHARD

No. You are as I've hoped. When we were

children

We swore to love forever.

ANNE

That was nonsense.

They say I'm to marry elsewhere.

RICHARD

Some great lord?

ANNE

Yes. *(There is a silence between them.)*

RICHARD

Now that I see you there's so much to say —

And I have no words. Anne! My dear one!

Anne!

ANNE

And I have none. *(Her figure has begun to fade, and

now suddenly it's gone. Richard steps toward

where she was. She's not there.)*

RICHARD

Anne! *(He turns to Dag.)* Dag, you must bring

her back! Dag!

Why did she go?

DAG

You spoke words not said at that time.

RICHARD

But I don't remember!

I don't remember the words said long ago!

Would she know them?

DAG

No. But when they are wrong

There's nothing to hold the hour together. It

goes

And she goes with it.

RICHARD

Dag, if you ever loved her,

	Bring her back for a moment! Only to see her!
	Only to say — !
DAG	What would you say, my master?
RICHARD	Something for her only! But quickly, while
	She's still near us! I have something to tell her
	That she died not knowing!
DAG	Would you say something new?
	Something not said in your lives?
RICHARD	Yes.
DAG	But that can't be.
	We can only call back old times.
RICHARD	But she died not knowing —
DAG	You can say only what was said before —
RICHARD	Who wants his life again if it's to be
	Unchanged? Who wants it the way it was?
DAG	We have come, my lord, to show it the way it
	was —
	Because of the lies about you —
RICHARD	To show it to these? *(He indicates the audience.)*
DAG	Yes.
RICHARD	Fool! Oh, fool! Fool!
	What do I care
	How it seems to them?
	They sit in an age I don't know
	Out there, out of time, out of space, too, out
	Of my life or yours or my lady's!
	I don't know them! Can't! They don't touch me!
	What they believe
	Is less than the ant that gnaws at my knuckle-
	bones!
	(To the audience.) (That's bad sometimes, that
	Ant. In case you've wondered

What it's like for a ghost who feels the nip
Of mandibles on his bones! It's bad,
And it's worse in sunny weather!)
Look, my jester,
Descendant of Merlin, or whoever he was,
This is why I must see my lady;
After she died,
And I had buried her,
I was too dull with grief to face my nobles—
So I let them wait,
And sat for a day among the things she left,
Her work-box and the dresses she had worn
And jewels—
And the small secret things a woman puts
Aside when a man comes in—
Still with her perfume light upon them.—
So there I found a letter written to me
To be opened after her death.
"For my dear Richard. To be opened when I
          am dead."
Inside it went something like this:
That because our son was dead and now it
          seemed
We'd have no more children,
For she was ill,
She wanted me to know that when she died
I was to marry again—and have an heir
To the throne.
And since my niece, Elizabeth,
The daughter of my brother, looked at me
With happiness in her eyes,
Perhaps I'd turn to her, be happier there

Than with unhappy Anne. And then she
    signed it,
"Anne, your Anne,
Who is sorry that she failed you,
And loves you wholly,
And will love you when she is gone."
Now, I tell you, Dag, my girl had never failed
    me,
Nor had I ceased to love her,
Nor looked at any woman, least of all
At Elizabeth, my niece.

DAG   Who told her this —
About Elizabeth?

RICHARD   I never knew
For I was away with one war after another,
Risings, rebellions,
Red rose and white,
Gules on a green field, gules on black,
Battles and carrion, death —
And I never knew
She was unhappy. I must tell her now —
I must tell her if I see her! I don't know
Your rules of necromancy, of how I must say
Only what was said before, and suchlike mat-
    ters,
This cannot hold me when I know she died
Thinking I no longer loved her!

DAG   These are not my rules, my lord,
But the rules of what can happen. Try if you
    wish.
Speak words that were not spoken. Tell her
    your love

Was the same at the end. She won't hear this.
    She will dim
And you will lose what you have.
My king, my sovereign,
Only the living can change. You and your
    queen
Have long been dead. The errors
Made in your lives can't be rescinded now.
There are the living. What is in their minds
Can still be altered. If they've been unjust
They'd want to alter it.
Let us bring back the past—
We can do no more—
So they can deal more justly with your name
Than they do now.

RICHARD   I take no pleasure in it.
It doesn't matter what they believe. Nor
    whether
It's true or untrue.

DAG   But I say it does! The truth
Does matter! I want them to know the truth
About my lord and my lady!
When a man's maligned,
When a name's blackened unjustly,
It shakes the order of things,
Sets a virulence working like the plague
At the bottom of a spring—
Sets a precedent of disease—
So all men are in danger!
If a lie is a lie, and you know it
And let it live, it corrupts every truth you know
Till truth begins to be lies!

RICHARD   But the lies about me,

What harm have they done except to me and
     my lady

In these times about us?

DAG   They have only encouraged all lies,

And liars about all men!

Just in so far

As history is a lie no man is safe

Whether he be alive or dead!

RICHARD   Let us do what we can.

In these researches

Shall I see Anne again?

DAG   Yes. You will see her.

RICHARD   Could we call her now?

DAG   First we must call on a rodent,

One Henry Tudor,

Who doesn't wish to come, who comes because

He must, because he's called, but lurks in crypts

Like the rat he is, till he's cornered,

And must speak. *(A shadow flickers at the foot of
     the rear curtain.)*

My spell is on him. See, he shuffles there

Under the curtain, tries to run away.

There's your Henry Tudor.

RICHARD   I see only a shadow.

DAG   He tries to look like a shade there, like a
     nothing,

Like a king of spades, dancing,

Now on the curtain, now on the floor!

He won't come to rest till he's pinned against a
     wall!

Come, we must corner him!

RICHARD   Does this lead to Anne?

DAG   It will lead to Anne, if we can shake this rat
Till the truth shakes out of him!
*(They corner the shadow. It flits back and forth desper-
ately as they close in. Then we see that it is really a
little, thin man with a thin whisker and furtive rat
face. It shivers and snarls at them — a subhuman
sound. Dag gets it by the collar of its old coat, and
holds it.)*

THE RAT   *(Clicking its teeth.)* Ck, ck, ck, ck!

RICHARD   Is this Henry Tudor?

DAG   This is Henry the Seventh, of England. Quite
majestic,
Don't you think?
Did you speak, Your Majesty?

HENRY   Ck, ck! *(He covers his eyes.)* Ck, ck, ck, ck!

DAG   Yes, Your Majesty.
It is bright here. You never liked the light.
You preferred dark holes and passages.

HENRY   What is this? Who holds me? *(His voice is almost
a squeak.)*

DAG   You've been dragged out
To show yourself in public. Those you see
Are here to judge your ways. *(Henry looks out
sharply at the audience, and then turns with a
slow, cautious movement toward the rear.)*
There's no way out.
You'll stand and take it. *(He lets go of the coat.)*
Try to go out. You'll find
You can't.
*(Henry looks out again in the audience, and as he does
so begins to draw himself up to his full size.)*

HENRY
Ah—give me a moment to collect myself.

I am not— *(He pulls his clothes into shape.)*

DAG
Take your own time, my lord.

HENRY
Who are these again? *(Indicating the audience.)*

Are these my citizens?

DAG
They are citizens.

Not yours, I believe.

HENRY
I'm the victim of some trick. A trick.

Of the kind with which you entertained the
    court

When you were called on. *(He finds a crown some-
    where in his rags and dons it.)*

You are Dag, the fool. *(He is now speaking like a
    king.)*

You used to call men from their graves,

Old grave-stained fellows,

Stumbling back through their lives

For us to laugh at.

But this time I'm the victim. The sacrifice.

I was in my grave, I remember. Well-interred

And honored and at peace.

You will excuse me, gentlemen. I know this fool

Of old, and his sleight-of-hand.

These are not my citizens?

DAG
No.

HENRY
Plain no? Not, no, my lord? Or if it please you?

DAG
Plain no.

HENRY
How many years have passed—to put it
    plainly—

Since I was buried? I see the fashions have
    changed.

DAG
I'm not good at arithmetic. I never

	Added up. It's been some time.
HENRY	Some time.
	Do they speak my language?
	The king's English?
DAG	With some changes.
HENRY	They can understand us?
DAG	Very well.
HENRY	And who is that?
DAG	You may remember Richard Plantagenet,
	Your predecessor.
HENRY	*(Under his breath.)* Richard.
RICHARD	My greetings, Henry.
HENRY	Will he be in this?
DAG	He will. This audience
	Will see you both in a few episodes
	That have been somewhat obscured.
HENRY	Will see us both?
DAG	Yes.
HENRY	I refuse to take part in such mumming!
DAG	But you will.
HENRY	I appeal to this court of inquiry! The fool's
	unfair!
	A friend of Richard's! He'll put me through
	Some plottery to cast doubt on what I did
	When I was king!
DAG	I shall put you through nothing,
	Can put you through nothing, that isn't the way
	it was.
	We shall see the events as they happened.
HENRY	I refuse!
DAG	You cannot refuse, as you know.
HENRY	I do refuse! *(He is suddenly the rat, as when first*

seen, trying to hide under the curtain, blinking at the light, scurrying back and forth. Dag and Richard corner him again, and he clicks at them; Richard catches him by the collar and shakes him hard. Henry stops struggling and suddenly climbs to his full height.)

DAG   That's better.

HENRY   *(facing Richard defiantly)* Why, good!

If you dare to show yourself to them,

You, Richard the Third, with your murders, rapes,

Throttlings, drownings, buryings alive, your poisons,

Tortures, ropes and chains, if you dare show your face,

Then I have nothing to hide! Let us proceed!

Let us show it all!

RICHARD   Yes, Henry. Just as it was

Let them see it all.

HENRY   They'll see this wild boar, this hog!

RICHARD   They'll see what was.

Dag, what day do we live?

DAG   First we must find

The day when Henry Tydder, the music master,

Taught Clarence and Bishop Morton a quick back way

To the throne of England.

HENRY   There was no such day!

DAG   My lord,

It will come back to you.

HENRY   Not if you were

	Merlin himself!
DAG	You will take your place, my lord. *(Reluctantly,*
	but as if unable to resist, Henry walks into the
	scene and is joined by Bishop Morton, an oily
	prelate. Clarence enters, meeting them.)
	See how it falls on them—
	A light more brilliant than reality,
	Like images in a glass, and when they speak
	The words come back, reflected. There, the
	light now,
	As sharp as childhood!
RICHARD	Anne is not here.
DAG	Not yet. *(He sits on the floor at stage left to watch the*
	episode. Richard kneels or crouches beside him.)
MORTON	I may see your wife, your grace?
CLARENCE	She's coming.
MORTON	How much is known
	About Richard and Anne? How far has it gone?
CLARENCE	They've been seen together.
	There was always a league between them.
MORTON	And it's renewed?
CLARENCE	Well, quite frankly, they were seen
	Lying on the grass under the great beech
	When the moon rose last night.
MORTON	Who saw them?
CLARENCE	Isabel.
MORTON	That could mean much or little.
CLARENCE	From other things
	That Isabel's observed, it's serious.
	They may be planning to marry.
MORTON	We agreed, your Lordship,
	That Anne must marry a commoner.

You were certain

You could keep her away from Richard.

CLARENCE   Well, I reckoned

Without my wife, or rather I counted on

Her vigilance, and *(Isabel enters)* she failed me.

There were no letters?

ISABEL   No, I swear it.

There were no letters, no messengers between
        them,

No communication before last night —

Then suddenly she was in his arms.

MORTON   You knew

That he was coming?

ISABEL   No — and she couldn't have known.

Yet there they were in the moonlight on the
        lawn,

And I thought she was in her room —

I'd heard no word of Richard. He came alone.

CLARENCE   Who let him in?

ISABEL   Anne must have.

CLARENCE   I lose half of Warwick's estates

If Richard marries Anne.

HENRY   You lose more than that.

MORTON   Listen.

HENRY   Keep Warwick's land

And Warwick's incomes, and you can make
        yourself king

Sooner or later. Give Richard half of it

And you're an earl, no more, never could be
        more

Than earl or duke.

CLARENCE   If she marries well she takes

<table>
<tr><td></td><td>One half as her marriage portion.</td></tr>
<tr><td>HENRY</td><td>Prevent it.</td></tr>
<tr><td>CLARENCE</td><td>How?</td></tr>
<tr><td>HENRY</td><td>A death or two might help.</td></tr>
<tr><td>CLARENCE</td><td>Whose?</td></tr>
<tr><td>HENRY</td><td>Richard's — Anne's.</td></tr>
<tr><td>CLARENCE</td><td>No.</td></tr>
<tr><td>HENRY</td><td>One or two deaths now may help as much
As ten thousand later.</td></tr>
<tr><td>MORTON</td><td>Perhaps you don't want it much.
Or not that much.</td></tr>
<tr><td>CLARENCE</td><td>I'd rather not murder for it.</td></tr>
<tr><td>HENRY</td><td>You don't want it much. Well, put her away
In some safe place. Though no place is quite safe
Except the one you shrink from.</td></tr>
<tr><td>MORTON</td><td>You must take her from him
And keep them apart.</td></tr>
<tr><td>CLARENCE</td><td>I agree to that.</td></tr>
<tr><td>HENRY</td><td>At once.</td></tr>
<tr><td>CLARENCE</td><td>Yes. At once.</td></tr>
<tr><td>HENRY</td><td>He must not see her again.
You have possession of Anne. Can she be put
Where Richard won't find her?</td></tr>
<tr><td>CLARENCE</td><td>Leave that to me.</td></tr>
<tr><td>MORTON</td><td>But make sure.</td></tr>
<tr><td>CLARENCE</td><td>As sure as death.</td></tr>
<tr><td>HENRY</td><td>Nothing's as sure as death.
She should be thrown
On a kitchen midden, like a dead cat. And covered
With what they throw from kitchens.</td></tr>
</table>

CLARENCE　　She will be. *(The lights go out on the scene, leaving
Dag and Richard alone on the stage.)*

RICHARD　　Isabel saw us
There on the lawn.

DAG　　It seems so.

RICHARD　　I rode up in the night
Without warning. The castle gates were closed.
I sat there on my horse, not wanting
To wake the household.
The moon came up, and I heard somebody
clanking
With bolts and chains.
It was Anne letting me in. Could we have that
scene?

DAG　　We're past it.

RICHARD　　Yes. But to hold her again—
As she was then. Oh, Dag, let it be moonlight
On that one night, and Anne there!

DAG　　Yes, master.
*(A shaft of cool moonlight comes across the curtains, as
if finding a way through the trees. There is a rattling
of chains and the sound of heavy bars falling. Richard
steps to stage left and then comes into the moonlight and
waits. Anne appears as a door swings open. She takes
a step toward him; he hesitates.)*

RICHARD　　Anne?

ANNE　　Dickon?

RICHARD　　Were you awake?

ANNE　　I woke and looked out the window.
I could see a horseman under the trees—
Somehow I knew you.

RICHARD　　I have only this hour.

<table>
<tr><td></td><td>I must be at the ford at sunrise.</td></tr>
<tr><td></td><td>The king expects me.</td></tr>
<tr><td>ANNE</td><td>More wars, more battles?</td></tr>
<tr><td>RICHARD</td><td>There's a castle to take.</td></tr>
<tr><td></td><td>Then I'll be free.</td></tr>
<tr><td>ANNE</td><td>I'm beginning to be afraid here.</td></tr>
<tr><td>RICHARD</td><td>You? Afraid here?</td></tr>
<tr><td>ANNE</td><td>Yes.</td></tr>
<tr><td>RICHARD</td><td>Of whom?</td></tr>
<tr><td>ANNE</td><td>Your brother. My sister.</td></tr>
<tr><td>RICHARD</td><td>Clarence?</td></tr>
<tr><td>ANNE</td><td>Yes.</td></tr>
<tr><td>RICHARD</td><td>But why?</td></tr>
<tr><td>ANNE</td><td>It's nothing that I can say.</td></tr>
<tr><td></td><td>Just that I feel it around me.</td></tr>
<tr><td>RICHARD</td><td>Isabel?</td></tr>
<tr><td></td><td>And Clarence?</td></tr>
<tr><td>ANNE</td><td>Yes.</td></tr>
<tr><td>RICHARD</td><td>My brother's wooly-minded,</td></tr>
<tr><td></td><td>But I never thought him dangerous.</td></tr>
<tr><td>ANNE</td><td>He is.</td></tr>
<tr><td>RICHARD</td><td>May I kiss you?</td></tr>
<tr><td>ANNE</td><td>Yes. (They kiss.)</td></tr>
<tr><td>RICHARD</td><td>You're cold.</td></tr>
<tr><td>ANNE</td><td>Oh, Dickon!</td></tr>
<tr><td></td><td>It's good to have you! You were away so long!</td></tr>
<tr><td>RICHARD</td><td>You're afraid.</td></tr>
<tr><td>ANNE</td><td>Not so much of Clarence or Isabel.</td></tr>
<tr><td></td><td>It's those around them.</td></tr>
<tr><td></td><td>The bishop and the little music-master —</td></tr>
<tr><td></td><td>Who knows no music.</td></tr>
<tr><td>RICHARD</td><td>They're both here?</td></tr>
</table>

ANNE   Both here.

RICHARD   This is Monday night—

            Or Tuesday morning. I could come for you
                Thursday

            At this same time. There'll be no moon.

ANNE   I know. Where would you take me?

RICHARD   We shall be married.

ANNE   And the king?

RICHARD   He'll say yes to us. Since this last battle

            He likes me well. He led the center and I—

            I led the right wing.

ANNE   You, Dickon?

RICHARD   We work well together.

            At any rate we won. We can count on the king.

            And I'll take you out of this.

            Let's sit here a moment.

ANNE   Do you have time?

RICHARD   Let the king wait.

            He can swim or eat breakfast.

            I must kiss my girl.

ANNE   Not here. Out of the moonlight.

            I was awake and someone else might be.

RICHARD   Is there someone doesn't like me?

ANNE   Doesn't like us together perhaps.

RICHARD   I don't know why. *(They sit.)*

ANNE   And I don't.

RICHARD   You're shivering.

            I'll put an arm about you.

            And from now on you shall have my arm when
                you need it.

ANNE   I need it now.

RICHARD   And will you marry me?

ANNE   I'll be waiting for you.

                I'm lost without you, Dickon.

                Come for me soon.

RICHARD   Let's set the time so there's no mistake.

                Two or three hours after midnight, Thursday

                    morning,

                Look for a horseman there, under the trees;

                Be ready to ride with me.

ANNE   I'll bring very little.

RICHARD   Bring yourself, sweet.

                I'll have four walls somewhere in the north of

                    England,

                With the usual bric-a-brac.

                It's a house to live in. It's ours.

ANNE   Thursday morning,

                Two or three hours after midnight.

                I won't sleep. I'll watch for you.

                *(They kiss. The lights go out on them and come up on
                Dag, sitting cross-legged at the side of the stage. Rich-
                ard comes toward him out of the darkness.)*

RICHARD   Did I leave to join the king?

DAG   It's your memory.

RICHARD   Yes, she went in,

                And I joined the king at the ford.

                When we had taken the castle I came back

                To keep our tryst, Thursday morning.

                The house was silent.

DAG   Stand under the trees

                And wait. It will come back to you.

RICHARD   *(Going to his place.)*

                But if this is the Thursday morning I won't see

                    Anne.

She never came.

There's no point in the scene without her.

DAG   Master, master, please remember we're here

To clear your name! Your love for Anne is
        over.

We and our loves are dead as Agememnon

Or the father of Agamemnon.

RICHARD   I've read my Homer.

The father of Agamemnon lived to be

An old man, shrunken; probably he looked

As old as God. But Agamemnon died

At midway, full of blood. That's true of me.

I died in battle when I was thirty-two,

My wife died at twenty-nine.

Do you wonder that I'm restless in my grave?

I never lived my life out. When I died

My love, my years, my youth were sweet in my
        mouth—

I reach out for them yet. And reach out for
        Anne.

DAG   You will see her again.

RICHARD   But my part in this scene is only to wait?

DAG   Only to wait.

*(Richard sits to watch and listen. Anne comes in si-
lently at stage right, out of his view, and seems to
swing a door open. A chain falls. Henry comes in
behind her and beckons to two men who follow.
Henry indicates Anne, who is about to go out through
the door when one of the men catches her from behind,
one of his hands covering her mouth to prevent a
scream. There is a scuffle as she is dragged off, stage
right. Richard leaps up but can see none of this and*

when it is quiet again resumes his seat, still watching.
When he can no longer bear the suspense he strides to
the door and raps sharply. The door is opened by
Clarence.)

CLARENCE Well, little brother! What brings you clapping at my door in the middle of the night?

RICHARD I came to see Anne.

CLARENCE Anne? Anne has gone to London.

RICHARD When?

CLARENCE Why, some days ago.

RICHARD For what reason?

CLARENCE Since when did girls give reasons for their vagaries? She gave me none. But she left saying she was going to London. Some of my people were travelling up to town and she took it into her head to go with them.

RICHARD This is strange.

CLARENCE Is it? Come in, if you like. Look about her rooms.

RICHARD No. I'll go to London. *(He turns away.)*

CLARENCE And no sleep? Very well. *(The scene fades. Richard speaks to Dag.)*

RICHARD It was a weary year before I found her. But I did find her!

DAG And you will see her again.

(Al, the stage manager, comes on from stage right, looking up at the curtain.)

AL Try that curtain now, Charlie! I think we've got it!

CHARLIE *(Offstage)* Right.

Curtain

Act Two

(The warning bell rings and the curtain goes up as usual, showing the empty stage. Al comes out, distressed, and looks up at the ropes that control the curtain.)

AL   *(Calling to his assistant.)* Put another man on it, Charlie!

CHARLIE   *(Backstage.)* No good, Al! Looks like a square knot from here!

AL   Who pushed that buzzer?

CHARLIE   Not me!

LEGER   *(Coming from the rear of the audience.)* Al!

AL   Yes, sir. Yes, Mr. Leger.

LEGER   You didn't signal for the buzzer?

AL   No, sir.

LEGER   Take the curtain down.

AL   Charlie's trying to get it down right now, and there's the same tangle in the lines we had before.

LEGER   The same tangle?

AL   Yes, sir.

LEGER   Who touched the ropes? *(He joins Al on the stage.)*

AL   Nobody. Charlie's been watching like a hawk, and so have I.

            But the lines are twisted and the curtain won't budge.

Leger	Well, for God's— *(He pauses, in deference to the audience.)*
Al	Who was this Merlin, anyway. Was he real?
Leger	None of it's real—Merlin, Richard, Anne— none of it!
Al	I'm beginning to wonder. *(Kent enters from stage right.)*
Kent	Say, Al, is this phone back here out of order?
Al	—Why, no.—Which one?
Kent	Well, I've tried both—the one backstage here and the booth downstairs, and I can't get the police department.
Al	Do you have the number?
Kent	I've got both the number of the station and the private number of the commissioner and I've been trying both for the last half hour.
Leger	The booth downstairs is working. I used it just before curtain-time.
Kent	Well, all I can get on it is the toll operator, and she keeps giving me the police department in some God-forsaken small town in England—
Leger	England—?
Kent	Not New England—England! She keeps giving me the police in Chichester or some place like that, and when I tell her I want the New York chief, I get the chief of police in York! York, England! For a while I thought it was straightened out and I had the commissioner on the wire, but then it turned out I was talking to

the Lord Mayor of London and he was hopping mad because I'd got him out of bed at 2:30 A.M.!

AL But they wouldn't wake the Lord Mayor!

KENT That's who he said he was—so then I decided to go to the station by taxi, and the stage door's jammed—

LEGER That's never happened—

KENT The doorman was outside trying to get in and I was inside trying to get out and I guess I was pretty mad. I broke a panel. But it's still stuck.

AL I'll take a look. *(He goes out right.)*

KENT I want to say this to the audience. Ladies and gentlemen, it may be that we won't be able to give the Richard play as announced. I confess I'm somewhat baffled by what's been going on around here—and maybe I'm a little scared. I don't give up yet—I'm still going to try to reach the commissioner and, of course, we won't allow that door to remain closed. But personally it seems to me that the best I'll be able to do is go across the street for that drink. If any of you want to join me there I'll be glad to pick up the check. I understand there's a performance of some kind going on here. As far as I'm concerned, it can continue for a while. We'll see to that stage door.

LEGER I think maybe that drink is a good idea.

(Kent and Leger go backstage together. A butler out of

Richard III's time walks on pompously, followed by three young servant girls of the same period. The girls carry long spoons.)

CLINK

(The butler.) Now I have established with you what your wages are to be. They are to be one penny a day for each, and you are required to work here in the kitchen from sun-up till supper-time, which will be when the cook finds it convenient. There is to be no giggling, no whispering, and no following. If the men servants try to kiss you, beat them off with your spoons and report the case to me. Do not believe it is because you are good-looking that you are followed. These fellows we have about would follow any female, especially one that smells of grease, as you do, all three, because of the garments I gave you. Now you will have different work for each day, and each day I will tell you what the work is. Some days you will sort goose-feathers, choosing out down for the pillows of my lord and lady. Some days you will sweep this court-yard, beginning at the gate and ending at the kitchen. Today you will take each your spoon and you will skim the grease from the top of the great kettle and place it in a barrell. The kettle will boil all day, and you will skim all day, and tomorrow we shall make soap. And you must think your-

selves happy that you work in the city
house of the brother of the king, where
so much soap is made that three wenches
work all day to skim the grease for it.
Come hither, you.

1st Girl | *(Going to him.)* Yes, sir.

Clink | My name is Clink, and I am butler here in the house of the Duke of Clarence. What kind of face have you? *(He inspects her.)*

1st Girl | A plain face. It was good enough for my mother.

Clink | She was easily pleased. Pass on. Let me see yours.

2nd Girl | Yes, sir.

Clink | Show me the reverse. This side is not too appetizing. *(The girl turns round.)* No, I thank you. Let me see this last. *(The other girl comes forward.)* Now here is one to pattern by. Here is truthfully a good-looking kitchen-wench. Let me see your legs, for sometimes these pretty faces blind a man and he fails to note that they are beef-to-the-heels. *(He starts to lift her skirt. She strikes him with her spoon. He staggers back.)* Why do you do that?

Anne | *(The 3rd girl.)* Beat them off with your spoons, you said.

Clink | I am butler in the city house of the brother of the king! I think I may lift a girl's skirt without reproof!

Anne | Could we proceed with the skimming of grease from the pot?

CLINK   Why, yes. No girl conceals her legs without
                 reason. You are beef-to-the-heels, and
                 prefer to remain covered. Come with
                 me, all of you. The pot is boiling. *(He
                 starts out to stage right, but pauses, hearing
                 voices toward stage left.)* Precede me and
                 begin to skim. I hear the voice of my
                 master. *(The girls go out right.)*

CLARENCE   *(Offstage at left.)* But not the kitchen, brother!

RICHARD   *(Offstage.)* Brother, I must look in the kitchen also!
                 (He comes on stage, followed by Clarence.)
                 What part of the house is this?

CLARENCE   The butler's pantry.

RICHARD   *(To Clink.)* And who are you? *(Clink is silent, over-
                 whelmed with deference, open-mouthed.)*

CLARENCE   This my butler, a poor, honest, stupid soul.

RICHARD   C-C-C-Cl— *(He swallows and gives up.)*

CLARENCE   His name is Clink, and his brain-power is ob-
                 vious. Brother Richard, I take it in very
                 ill part that you come with armed men
                 to search my house!

RICHARD   *(To Clink.)* I want to see every woman who
                 works for you.
                 (Clink looks at Clarence.)

CLARENCE   You look for Anne among these frowsy slat-
                 terns?

RICHARD   I have sought her for more than a year, Clar-
                 ence, and she has been spirited from one
                 place to another. Today I have traced
                 her to your house. She is not upstairs;
                 She may be below-stairs.

CLARENCE   *(To Clink.)* Fetch the cook.

RICHARD	Fetch out every woman who works for you.
CLARENCE	Good. Fetch them. *(He turns.)* Good hunting to you. *(Clink goes out right.)*
RICHARD	Don't try to slip away, Clarence. Those are the king's soldiers about your house.
CLARENCE	Why are they here?
RICHARD	You were setting yourself up to be king, with the help of Bishop Morton and the little troubador. The stealing of Anne was only part of your scheme. Edward sent me to arrest you.
CLARENCE	I? You would arrest me?
RICHARD	The way you were playing it, it was your neck or brother Edward's. He prefers his own.
ISABEL	*(Outside, to the left.)* Clarence! Clarence! I am under arrest! *(She runs in, followed by a man-at-arms.)*
CLARENCE	And so am I, but not till little brother learns his lesson! *(He draws his sword, Richard draws and disarms Clarence.)*
RICHARD	Go with the captain.
CLARENCE	I make an ignoble ending. *(He and Isabel turn and go with the officer. Clink comes from the right, leading the three girls with long spoons.)*
CLINK	Here be three. *(Richard turns to him.)*
RICHARD	Three of what? Three who eat with the devil? Anne! Anne! *(He goes to her.)*
ANNE	*(Holding him off.)* I have my orders! No followers! "Beat them off with your long spoons," says he!
RICHARD	Anne! I've found you at last!

ANNE

Not in this dress, Richard! It's filthy to the floor! It stinks!

RICHARD

(His arms round her.) I bring a new dress for you, darling! This is our wedding day!

ANNE

Richard! Richard! I knew you'd find me! I've been skimming fat to make soap tomorrow! *(They go out with their arms round each other.)*

CLINK

So I'm stupid, am I? And you was a lady, the pretty one. I might have known when she held her petticoats down. *(The lights go out on the scene and come up on Dag, who is seen sitting at stage left. Richard goes up to him.)*

DAG

Have I kept my promise?

RICHARD

You have bettered it.

It all came out as it was, every word as it was.

DAG

You thought you couldn't remember.

RICHARD

Where has it lain, this old day? In what record book

Is it written down and pictured?

DAG

That I don't know. But somewhere it is,

The whole past, and can be called on.

RICHARD

What have you called

For our next scene?

DAG

Bishop Stillington.

RICHARD

You go fast.

That was an evil time, when I became king.

DAG

He's here, you see.

RICHARD

Yes, as he was. *(A bishop with a flowing beard and a lean ascetic face comes into the light. Richard approaches him in a flash of anger.)*

STILLINGTON — You have sent for me, my lord?

RICHARD — Why have you done this?

STILLINGTON — I am a man of God, my king. I serve

God first, and after God my king. I spoke

The truth.

RICHARD — Then you spoke it late!

STILLINGTON — I spoke in time.

RICHARD — Why not before?

STILLINGTON — My king, if I had told

While Edward was alive, and on the throne,

That he was a bigamist and his children bas-
        tards,

What would have happened to me?

RICHARD — You'd have lost your head.

But a man who serves God should be willing to
        lose his head

In that service.

STILLINGTON — And what would God have gained?

The queen would have had me killed, would
        have kept her place,

Her son would be king.

RICHARD — I would he were.

STILLINGTON — My lord,

Things are one way or another, true or not
        true,

As I see it. I married your brother, Edward
        Fourth,

To Eleanor Butler, some years before he mar-
        ried

Elizabeth Woodville. I've brought before Parlia-
        ment

The documents and witnesses to attest this,

And the Parliament, having no other course,
With the evidence before them, have decided
That Edward's children are base-born, and
    therefore
You must take the throne.

RICHARD   I was loyal to Edward,
Loyal to Edward's son. My loyalty
Has been my life.

STILLINGTON   Be loyal now to England.
For you are England's king. *(There is a horn call
    at stage right, and Anne is seen standing there
    in a white dress with a long train. She wears a
    gold crown. Two lords hold the train of her
    dress.)*

RICHARD   The coronation
Is not till tomorrow.

ANNE   It seems that kings and queens
Rehearse these paces. This is what I'm to wear
When we appear together. *(She comes to him.)*
    Oh, Richard, Richard,
Should a crown seem so heavy?

RICHARD   Does it seem so?

ANNE   Yes.
And there's something heavy here — and here.
Could we escape this? Couldn't we be as we
    were,
Let your nephew reign?

RICHARD   The bishop says no.

STILLINGTON   The parliament says no.

ANNE   I don't know why
But I think it will be evil.

RICHARD   I don't want it,

	Don't like it, and I think it will bring ill,
	But I don't know why.
STILLINGTON	You must rule England.
RICHARD	God help us.
STILLINGTON	Dear children,
	I think he will, and I think you will rule well.

(The lights go out on the scene, and come up on Dag as before. Richard speaks to him out of the darkness.)

RICHARD
There was never any gladness in it for her,
As there was sometimes for me. To know that
    laws
Were needed, like reforms in the jury system,
(He comes into the lights.)
More freedom for Caxton, the printer, better
    roads,
Some order among the couriers that carried
Letters and messages, things like this
Gave me a little happiness sometimes,
But never Anne. Perhaps she knew what waited
For us, behind the years. Does one ever know
What lies in wait?

DAG
I do. And since I do
Others may.

RICHARD
But nothing was really wrong
Till our son died. Then everything went wrong,
Everything together.
(The light comes up on Anne as she kneels in her regal finery over a white coffin.) Must we see that now,
Anne and our son gone? Show us the Christmas
    time
That came before. *(But Anne speaks.)*

ANNE
I kept him at Middleham.

I didn't want him spoiled like Edward's
    children,
And I was wrong. The physicians were better at
    court.
He was always delicate. They might have saved
    him.
They might have saved him. Oh, my little boy!
And I didn't want you spoiled! Edward! Ed-
    ward!
My little son!

RICHARD   Let us see the Christmas, Dag!
This all comes late, too late and out of order!
Why should I not see Anne and see my son
When he was alive and she was happy?
(The lights fade on Anne.)

DAG   My lord,
You will! I suppose it comes as one remem-
    bers—
Not always whole—or in order.

RICHARD   But that last Christmas.
Let's try to have it whole—not only Anne
And our son—but my brother Edward, who
    was king,
With his queen and their two sons.

DAG   That was the day
He chose you to be protector.

RICHARD   Was it that day?
Would you know that?

DAG   You told me of it later.
During the masque I watched you talking apart,
And you told me why.

RICHARD   Yes, it comes to mind now—

	And seems to come with music. Was there a

And seems to come with music. Was there a
    song?

DAG   "Oh, melancholy
Is the holly"—

RICHARD   "In the summertime." *(He muses a moment.)*
Dag, so far I've said
Only the words I was supposed to say
In the days called back. What would happen to
    her,
To Anne, if I said more?

DAG   You've seen it. She fades.

RICHARD   But in her heart—in her mind? What happens
    there?
Is it a hurt?

DAG   It's the bitterness of dying
To be suffered through again.
Or so it was
When it came first to me. Let her believe
That the hour is new.

RICHARD   Well—now the Christmas. The king was there,
    and the queen.

*(A Christmas carol begins in the darkness, a boy's voice
singing and a lute or cithern playing with him. As the
song proceeds the lights come up on the scene and Dag
is seen to be singing with the boy. Little Edward is
nine or ten, and singing for his father and mother,
Richard and Anne, who sit listening. With them are
King Edward IV and his queen, Elizabeth Woodville,
and their two children. Two servants stand in the
rear.)*

DAG & EDWARD   *The Holly Tree*
(singing)   "Back in the summertime

The sober holly tree
Was hung with berries green, oh,
     Green as they could be.
Oh, melancholy
Was the holly
     In the summertime!
But in the wintertime
     The merry holly tree
Is hung with berries red, oh,
     Red as they can be,
Oh, red and jolly
Is the holly
     In the winter rime!" *(Richard and Anne applaud.)*

EDWARD Master Dag, may I ask you a question?

DAG Master Edward, out of question you may.

RICHARD *(To Anne, low.)* What is this?

ANNE Don't interrupt. They've rehearsed it.

RICHARD Oh. *(He takes Anne's hand.)*

DAG Ask your question, Master Edward.

EDWARD Which hand do you use to eat with?

DAG Oh, I'm left-handed. I usually eat with my left hand.

EDWARD That's strange.

DAG What's strange about it?

EDWARD Well, I always eat with my mouth! Laugh, Mother, laugh!
That's the joke!

ANNE We're all laughing! Don't you hear us?

KING EDWARD We're roaring with mirth!

THE QUEEN Listen! Ha, ha, ha, ha, ha!

RICHARD The king is laughing! And the queen!

EDWARD	Oh, but that one's not so good! We have a much better one, don't we Dag?
DAG	Much better.
RICHARD	I like your singing, too.
EDWARD	Oh, but, listen! Master Dag, why was the princess blind?
DAG	Because the prince was handsome?
EDWARD	No.
DAG	Because she was bashful?
EDWARD	No, no! She was blind because when the prince came in she dropped her eyes! Laugh, Mother! *(Anne laughs.)*
ANNE	I'm laughing!
EDWARD	Is it funny?
THE KING	Ha, ha, ha! I shall do myself a mischief!
RICHARD	It's very funny. Dag, you have a pitiful influence on the prince's mind.
DAG	My lord, it was what he wanted.
EDWARD	I want to be a jester when I grow up.
RICHARD	Why not a warrior?
EDWARD	Because warriors know no music, and music is what I love. But now, if you will excuse me! *(Little Edward sits. Dag is seen speaking.)*
DAG	This year, in place of the Christmas masque, your highnesses, we have an entertainment out of old days. The conquerors of England will appear before us habited as in their life-times, and give us a glimpse of what was. Julius Caesar will appear, and William the Conqueror.
LITTLE EDWARD	Oh, I'll like that!

ANNE	Yes, but listen quietly.
THE KING	*(To Richard.)* Could I speak to you a moment?
RICHARD	Of course. *(The king and Richard walk together, the king's arm round Richard, to stage right, where they can speak aside.)*
THE KING	*(Indicating Dag's activities.)* Must we listen to this?
RICHARD	Not if there's something of importance to be said.
	It's Dag's usual Christmas pantomime.
THE KING	Does he really bring back folk out of history, or is it all acting and mystification?
RICHARD	The truth is I don't know. I don't think he could bring folk back.
THE KING	I don't either—This is what I wanted to speak about,—
	Two weeks ago I was struck down by something. For half a day I couldn't move my left side. Then it went away, but it hangs over me. It could be a portent.
RICHARD	My king—
THE KING	Call me brother. You've been the only man I could trust. The only man who can lead an army, and win, and take nothing for himself.
RICHARD	You have taken too little care of yourself. For the good of the state, you must live. Your sons are not old enough to manage England.
THE KING	If I should die—
RICHARD	There would be chaos.
THE KING	Nevertheless, I might die. And if I do I don't want my wife's relatives setting up a

	regency and managing England and the children. They're selfish, ambitious and unscrupulous, the lot of them.
RICHARD	What other course is there?
THE KING	I shall make you protector. With full powers to rule the kingdom during the children's minority.
RICHARD	My lord, —
THE KING	Brother, please —
RICHARD	My brother —
THE KING	*(Pointing to Dag.)* Look! He's brought Julius Caesar as he promised!

(In a pool of light, Julius Caesar is seen standing alone, in deep thought. He lifts his arms in a gesture of despair.)

DAG	When Julius Caesar had come to the end of what he could do in Britain, he decided, standing alone on the road to Scotland, that he must give up and turn back. This is that moment.

(Caesar, dropping his arms, turns back slowly, looking longingly over his shoulder.)

RICHARD	We could have told him the Scotch are hardly worth the trouble.
THE KING	Yes, we could, brother. But you've brought order to the Highlands, anyway for the present.
RICHARD	At least they're quiet.
THE KING	Lest we should not have time for this later, I've had an instrument drawn, making you Protector in the event of my death, and I hand it to you now. *(He gives Richard a*

                               rolled parchment.) A similar document is registered with the Parliament, so there could be no question of my intent.

RICHARD   You truly fear this?

THE KING   I truly fear what would happen if Rivers and Hastings — ah!

RICHARD   What is it?

THE KING   Look who appears! *(He points toward Dag and his group.)*

DAG   He who is seen now began many things; his blood runs in your veins, most of you. *(A figure begins to show in the pool of light.)* When William the Conqueror first landed in Britain the little boat that put in from his ship was washed up on a beach near Bristol. William leaped out onto the sand, but the receding wave took the boat and his followers out again. He was left alone and somewhat dampened on the shingle. *(William is seen, calling to his mariners.)*

WILLIAM   Holla! Holla! Que faites-vous? Cochons! Malheureux!

                               (The figure fades and vanishes.)

THE KING   *(To Richard.)* Keep this safe, brother.

RICHARD   I shall keep it safe, my king.

DAG   And now for the end, Your Majesties, we have a dance of our own devising.

ANNE   *(To the King and Richard.)* Richard! Edward! Couldn't business come a little later? Couldn't you watch the ending?

THE KING   Ah, forgive us, Anne, let us see the dance! *(The King and Richard return to their seats.)*

DAG & EDWARD   *(Singing and dancing as they sing.)*
But in the winter-time,
    The merry holly tree,
Is hung with berries red, oh,
    Red as they can be!
Oh, red and jolly
Is the holly
    In the winter rime!
(The lights go out on the scene. Richard speaks out of the darkness.)

RICHARD   This was his last Christmas, and her last.
No more music. For him or for her or for me,
No more music.
And yet, she loved me too.
Why did it seem to her that life was empty
After our son was gone? I loved my lady.
How could she believe that I loved elsewhere?
What put this in her mind?

DAG   You were away in battle.
And a woman came to stay with her, a woman
Sent by Bishop Morton. And therefore sent
By Henry. In that last illness they spent long
    hours
Together. This woman and Anne.

RICHARD   Sent by Morton?

DAG   And Henry.

RICHARD   Even then—even then!

DAG   But that was later too.
You were in Scotland when your brother died,
Leaving the throne to his little son. It all

Came about as Edward feared. A swarm of
              uncles
And brothers-in-law took power.
(The lights come up on a scene in which the Queen
[Elizabeth] is surrounded by Lords Rivers, Hastings,
Stanley and Grey, and consulting with Bishop Morton
and Henry Tudor.)

MORTON   You are the queen. Your son is the king of
              England,
Or will be when he's crowned. No duke on
              earth
Can take this from you.

ELIZABETH   But Richard is protector;
My husband made a will to this effect
And the Parliament has the will.

HENRY   If I may speak—

ELIZABETH   *(Grudgingly.)* Yes, surely.

HENRY   Madam, the duties of a protector,
It's a question what they are—and legally
You can challenge his right to be guardian of
              your son—
A mother should care for her child. Well, this
              takes time,
And while the courts are thinking the matter
              over
You can make the kingdom yours.

ELIZABETH   But the Parliament,
Will it wait for the courts?

HENRY   It must wait. Your husband himself
Taught it to honor the judges.

RIVERS   Let us delay
The coronation, consolidate the power

	In our own hands.
HENRY	And when Richard arrives
	Let him protect himself, if he's protector.
ELIZABETH	Delay the coronation?
HENRY	Till the boy's crowned
	You will rule England.
	(A servant looks in.)
THE SERVANT	Madam?
ELIZABETH	Yes?
THE SERVANT	The Duke of Gloucester's here, and—
RIVERS	Richard!
MORTON	Good God,
	What shall we do with him?
HENRY	It's simple enough.
	The queen must refuse to see him.
RIVERS	Yes.
ELIZABETH	Since he's here
	I think I must admit him.
HENRY	Then promise him nothing,
	Commit yourself to nothing.
ELIZABETH	Tell the duke
	That he may enter.
THE SERVANT	Yes, Madam. *(He goes out.)*
HENRY	*(Turning away.)* I won't be here.
MORTON	Nor I.
ELIZABETH	You'll stay and face him, all of you!
	If he's to be feared, and I'm to hold him off
	Then stay and help me do it!
HENRY	Well, if you wish it.
ELIZABETH	I wish it! And if Bishop Morton is one of us
	Let him be seen here!
MORTON	Very well.

THE SERVANT	*(Reentering.)* The Duke of Gloucester!
ELIZABETH	Let him come in.
	(The servant steps aside and Richard comes into the presence of the queen, taking in the ring of advisors about her.)
RICHARD	My duty to you, Elizabeth.
ELIZABETH	I thank you, Richard.

RICHARD	And to all these about you
	My friendly greetings.
	This was sad news that caught me
	On the Scotch border. The queen has lost a
	    husband
	Whom she loved, and who loved her. I have
	    lost
	A brother, who was my close friend. We, all of
	    us,
	Have lost a king whom we can ill spare, a king
	Who wore the light of genius on him, a light
	To make men follow. Let us hope his son
	Will wear it when he's grown.

ELIZABETH	You are named Protector. When should my son be crowned?
RICHARD	At once.
ELIZABETH	Those about me advise delay.
MORTON	There must be some pause—
RIVERS	Some preparation.
RICHARD	But why?
ELIZABETH	There must of course be time for fitting cos- tumes, And sending out invitations.
RICHARD	Yes, for such things We must wait some days, perhaps.

MORTON	How long?
RICHARD	*(To Elizabeth.)* You would know this better than I.
ELIZABETH	What date is in your mind?
RICHARD	Why, this is the eighth of June; Two weeks should be enough. On June twenty- second We should make your son king.
MORTON	I think I see your plan. You mean to crown the lad so that you, as Pro- tector, May govern the kingdom.
RICHARD	That is my intention. And that was my brother's intent when he made the will. I shall try to carry it out.
MORTON	You intend to govern?
RICHARD	I do.
HENRY	Then, madam, when your son's crowned This duke will act as king.
RICHARD	But only during The king's minority.
ELIZABETH	When he comes of age You would resign as Protector?
RICHARD	I will resign — Exactly as directed in Edward's will.
RIVERS	This I do not believe.
MORTON	Nor I.
HENRY	Nor I.
ELIZABETH	*(To Henry.)* Who are you to speak in this pres- ence? The son of a son Of an obscure Welsh noble who married a widow

Who was once married to a king! Does this
Give you a voice here?

HENRY   I'm sorry, madam. I'm here
Only to advise my friend.

ELIZABETH   I don't trust your friend,
And I don't trust you! I have more faith in
     Richard!
If he says he will resign the power he will!
I'm quite certain you would not!

RIVERS   Madam, we agreed—

ELIZABETH   I agreed to nothing!
Of all the men about him
The king put most faith in Richard!
I shall trust him!
Let us set an immediate date for the coronation,
As Richard advises!

RIVERS   You will lose the help
Of the nobles who stand round you; mine, for
     one!

MORTON   And mine!

HENRY   And mine!

RIVERS   Yes, every man here present
Will be lost to you!

ELIZABETH   Why?

MORTON   Would you give up power
When it's in your hands?

ELIZABETH   I think it's safer
In Richard's hands than yours! And Edward
     thought so
When he chose Richard!

RIVERS   If you choose Richard now
I warn you plainly, there will be war!

RICHARD   Lord Rivers,
                I shall speak plainly, too. The knot of men
                That clusters about the queen there — uncles,
                        brothers,
                Hangers-on — you have made up your minds to-
                        gether
                To cling to the boy king, rule through him.
                        This was not
                What Edward wanted. He made me Protector
                To guard against just that. And I shall try
                To carry out his wish. If you go to war
                This will tear England!
                You have no legal claim —
                Only a hold on offices and powers
                Which you don't want to lose. You've held them
                        long
                But that does not mean you own them.
                It would be far better
                To give up these powers and keep the peace.
MORTON   Give up
                Your powers then! Your power as Protector.
                I tell you we don't trust you!
RICHARD   It's well known
                That you're a man to be trusted, Bishop Mor-
                        ton.
                The queen has made her choice. *(To Elizabeth.)*
                Do they hold your son?
ELIZABETH   No. He's safe from them. *(She comes over to
                        Richard.)*
RICHARD   We must take our plans for the coronation.
RIVERS   Leave me out of the plans.
RICHARD   Very well.

MORTON   One true thing you said:

                "This will tear England."

RICHARD   Let me revise what I said.

                You will tear England! *(The scene darkens. Richard*
                        is seen speaking with Dag.)

                Yes, it was that way.

                Or something like it. How it went on from
                        there

                I don't recall. Reality's so confused —

                Motives, cross-purposes, irrelevant details;

                In fact, it's nearly all irrelevant

                Compared with a play.

DAG   The boy was never crowned.

RICHARD   No. Shortly after this Bishop Stillington

                Went to Parliament with his news.

DAG   I was at the palace

                When a herald came to Elizabeth.

                (There is a sudden fanfare of trumpets, and Elizabeth
                is seen with her women. A servant appears at the
                door.)

THE SERVANT   Madam —

ELIZABETH   Whose horns are these?

THE SERVANT   Madam —

ELIZABETH   Tell them to cease this blaring! Tell me his
                        name

                When the noise ends! *(The trumpets are silenced.)*

THE SERVANT   Madam, it's only a herald

                Sent by the Parliament.

ELIZABETH   He could come in less rudely.

                What does he want?

THE SERVANT   To deliver a message.

ELIZABETH   Why, then,

	Let him come in with it.
THE SERVANT	Yes, madam, He's here.

(The servant steps outside and a herald in full panoply enters. Coming before the queen, he lifts the horn to his lips.)

ELIZABETH No, no! No more of that! We heard you come
        in
And we know you're here. You can put
Your noise away
And deliver your speech.

HERALD Madam, I come to read
A message from the Parliament!

ELIZABETH Read and be done,
I beg of you.

HERALD *(Lifting a scroll and reading.)*
From the Parliament of England,
Greetings!
Greetings to Elizabeth, who sat
Beside Edward as his queen, before his death,
And when he was king of this island.
Whereas Bishop Robert Stillington of Bath
Has come before the Lords and Commons, sitting
Together, and has laid before them proofs
That Edward was married to Lady Eleanor
        Butler
Daughter of the first Earl of Shrewsbury,
Married to her before he married you,
Elizabeth,
Therefore his children by you are all base-born,
Born out of wedlock, and cannot inherit,
Cannot inherit land, property, name or throne
Of the aforesaid Edward!

A WOMAN   What's that? What's that?

ELIZABETH   Is this a dream? Is this
              Happening to me?

A WOMAN   This cannot be true!

ANOTHER   Does he come from the Parliament?

ANOTHER   He says he does.

HERALD   I have more to read.

ELIZABETH   It can be no less welcome that what you've
                  read.
              Read on.

HERALD   Whereas King Edward left no heir
              Among his children, the throne of England
                  passes
              To his next of kin, his brother —

A WOMAN   To his brother?

HERALD   To his next of kin, his brother, the Duke of
                  Gloucester,
              Who is called to accept the throne, and will be
                  when crowned,
              Richard the Third of England!

ELIZABETH   Let me see that paper!

HERALD   *(Showing his scroll.)* I am sent by the Lords and
                  Commons.

ELIZABETH   Unless this is a most elaborate fraud
              It seems to be true. They sent him.

A WOMAN   But this news —

ELIZABETH   I don't believe it. He was a careless man
              Where women were concerned, but not that
                  careless.

HERALD   I may take my leave?

ELIZABETH   You've done your harm. You may go. *(The
                  herald goes.)*

Who is this Bishop of Bath, this Stillington,
Who seems to speak for the devil? When I was
      lowest,
When I thought all was lost, and life was over
I never imagined this! Send for him! God!
It may be true! Send for this Stillington!
(The lights darken on the scene, revealing Dag, where
he sat in a corner, watching the episode. Richard
speaks to him.)

RICHARD   You saw this?

DAG   Yes—and remember it.

RICHARD   And it turned out to be true—
The king had been careless,
Or worse,
And left no heir among his children,
And I was king.
Dag, why did I lose at Bosworth?
I had never lost a battle, and Bosworth field
Should have been mine.

DAG   You were betrayed, my lord.
Stanley betrayed you.
Half your army marched around to fight against
      you
Under Lord Stanley's orders.
(A light comes up on Henry, Stanley, Rivers, Grey and
Morton, bearing arms.)

STANLEY   What am I offered?

HENRY   Are you so blunt?

MORTON   Why, good,
Let him be blunt if he likes! We offer more
Than you'll get from Richard.

STANLEY   Richard's an honest man. I'll get nothing from him

That I haven't got already.

HENRY
What do you say

To Warwick's estates in the north of England, and

The name of Earl?

STANLEY
Warwick's estates are nothing.

For the name of earl, for that I'd do a good deal.

HENRY
Would you change sides?

STANLEY
When?

HENRY
In the midst of a battle. When you're counted on.

STANLEY
Let's talk about it.

(The light darkens on the scene, comes up again on Richard and Dag.)

RICHARD
Anne had warned me against him.

Our son was dead, and she

Was dying, though I didn't know it then.

I remember our last words together.

There was a woman with her, as you said,

Before I came.

(The lights come up on a couch where Anne is lying, pale and quiet. A woman sits beside her holding her hand.)

ANNE
I cannot believe

But that he loves me still.

ALISON
(The woman.) We must remember

How selfish a love is, even in those who love

Most deeply. The illness of a wife

Sometimes seems to an adoring husband

Like an infidelity — a turning away

From his love for her.

ANNE	I have been ill.
ALISON	And it is
	A turning away.
ANNE	But not an unfaith! I love him!
ALISON	There's a cool selfishness in men that looks
	At life with hard eyes; it's in both men and
	kings,
	But most in kings. It looks at sickness and death
	As human conduct, conduct that we choose.
	Sickness is failure, death is departure.
ANNE	Richard,
	Richard, have I failed you?
ALISON	You must not die,
	For if you die that's a real perfidy
	To your king, your husband.
ANNE	It would be better, though.
	He could love elsewhere.
ALISON	We think when we're in love
	That we're not replaceable, but it's not true;
	No, when we're gone it's nature's way for a man
	To look about him.
ANNE	If I were gone, and Richard
	Looked about, he'd see Elizabeth.
ALISON	Yes.
	And others. There are others who look at him.
ANNE	She follows him with her eyes; then when he
	leaves
	The room she's restless. After a while she makes
	Her excuses cleverly, and goes.
ALISON	Yes.
ANNE	But he never sees her, never!
ALISON	Your son is dead. In a king unfaith

Is sometimes a virtue. To be true to his kingdom
Richard must have a son.

ANNE   Help me up! *(She tries to rise. Alison helps her.)*
My breath came hard for a moment. It will
pass.
Oh God! Oh Richard!

RICHARD   *(At the doorway.)* Anne, did you call my name?

ANNE   Richard, Richard!
You were away so long!

RICHARD   So many things—
There's an invasion pending. I must ready for
that,
And there's money to raise. Sweet, it's been
long for me too,
Long, long, long, and needless!

ANNE   *(Her arms round him.)* More wars?

RICHARD   That little fellow
The music master, has made a claim to be king
In my place—

ANNE   He—king of England?

RICHARD   Little Henry,
The one who stayed with Morton. His claim to
the throne
Is baseless, yet the man has some sinister
power,
He fills the air with evil.

ANNE   His face is evil.

RICHARD   He's being supported
By some powerful nobles, and the king of
France
Lends him an army.

ANNE	I thought we'd have peace at last.
RICHARD	We should. We've earned it.
	Yet if he lands on the coast
	With any force, I'll have to fight him off—
	And that means money and soldiers.
ANNE	And you away,
	Always away. Could you stay with me,
	Richard?
	Till the winter ends? Your name alone should
	defeat
	This tinkling Tudor.
RICHARD	No, he does have the Welsh
	Behind him, and he's promising anything
	To those who'll follow. He can make great
	promises,
	Any wild gift, since he's not on a throne
	And doesn't have to pay. It's not like fighting
	With a man, it's like fighting with a rat, a rat
	Whose bite is venomous.
ANNE	*(Suddenly turning to him.)* Richard, his mother!
	Henry's mother!
RICHARD	Yes?
ANNE	She's married to Stanley,
	Steward of your household!
RICHARD	He's an honest man.
ANNE	But married to that woman! Oh, my dear,
	You've been too trusting. You forgave her when
	She plotted with Hastings against you, let her
	keep
	Her lands and titles! Now her son invades
	And she's married to your steward!
RICHARD	I know the woman,

	But I trust Lord Stanley.
ANNE	And Stanley's brother
	Is chamberlain of North Wales! Oh, what would happen
	If they went over to Henry?
RICHARD	If they changed sides
	Even Henry would have a chance. But the Stanleys have
	No reason to betray me.
ANNE	You must see to this quickly!
RICHARD	Darling, you're not well. Your cheeks are hectic,
	And your eyes too bright for health.
ANNE	But you must see to it!
	She's not to be trusted!
RICHARD	I'll not leave you tonight.
ANNE	Oh, what you must do
	You must do! I must sometimes be lonely!
	I can bear that!
RICHARD	This illness is no light thing.
	It recurs too often.
ANNE	Dickon, I'm foolish and sad—
	Not ill. You'll never find me ill again,
	I promise you! Don't waste an hour with me!
	You have a king's work to do!
RICHARD	Not ill?
ANNE	Not ill! *(She rises.)*
	Kiss me and then tend, if you must,
	To this singer and his Stanleys! I will not
	Lie a-bed when you come back!
RICHARD	That's a promise?
ANNE	A promise that I'll keep! Your wife will be

<table>
<tr><td></td><td>All new when you return! (They kiss. The lights go out, showing Anne looking after him. Richard speaks from the darkness.)</td></tr>
<tr><td>RICHARD</td><td>When I returned
It was to find Anne gone. She died believing
I could love quickly elsewhere, take another
    wife
All new. Must she lie there believing this
As long as earth is earth?</td></tr>
<tr><td>DAG</td><td>I think she must.</td></tr>
<tr><td>RICHARD</td><td>I won't go back quietly to my grave
And leave it so.</td></tr>
<tr><td>DAG</td><td>Well. We return to Henry.</td></tr>
<tr><td>KENT</td><td>(Calling from the rear of the auditorium.) Leger! Mr. Leger!</td></tr>
<tr><td>AL</td><td>(Looking out.) He's backstage, Mr. Kent.</td></tr>
<tr><td>KENT</td><td>I'll come back. The squad's on its way. It took a little time. — Are these shadows still operating?</td></tr>
<tr><td>AL</td><td>They're doing pretty well for shadows. Certainly nothing like Richard Third. (Leger and Al go backstage.)</td></tr>
<tr><td>RICHARD</td><td>Let Henry lie. Peace to him.</td></tr>
<tr><td>DAG</td><td>No. Bear in mind
You're dead when this next scene happens. It's after Bosworth.
You've been betrayed by the Stanleys, and defeated
And killed. Dear Henry's king, the music man
Who has no music.</td></tr>
<tr><td>RICHARD</td><td>Your rules don't fit together,
Descendent of Merlin! When you recall old Henry</td></tr>
</table>

       Things are said that weren't said when he lived,

       And the same with me! Why can't I speak to
         Anne

       As you speak to me — or Henry? Whose rules
         are these?

       Who made these rules?

DAG   I don't know.

RICHARD   But you know what they are!

DAG   My lord,

       There are no rules at all.

RICHARD   Then you make rules,

       And you choose how to call Anne!

DAG   Choose?

RICHARD   Yes, magician!

       I've trusted you as a friend, but now I see

       Some kind of malevolence in the way you
         dangle

       Your grave-yard puppets! You will have your
         show as you want it,

       And the puppets will speak as instructed! Not
         otherwise!

       Is it so?

DAG   No. No, master.

RICHARD   Then explain it.

DAG   Master, there is darkness in every mind

       That no eye has seen into. Do you know

       All that's in your mind?

RICHARD   No.

DAG   Master, truly,

       I can't control what I want and whom I call for,

       Some things I cannot do!

RICHARD   What can't you do?

Dag

> Master, forgive me. This same darkness in me,
> I think it doesn't want my mistress to know
> You were not unfaithful. Would rather she be-
>   lieved
> She'd lost you.

Richard

> Why? What do you gain by this?

Dag

> Loss? Gain? Is there ever any loss or gain
> For the demons in that subterranean chasm
> Where we do our thinking?

Richard

> It's because you love her.

Dag

> One could put it so.

Richard

> And I cannot say to Anne
> Any new thing?

Dag

> I've tried to change this. I can't.
> There's something in me that won't. Forgive
>   me!

Richard

> Yes.

Dag

> And may I deal now with Henry?

Richard

> Lad, if you love her
> So deeply you must know why I cry out, here
> On this alien stage, in this alien land, in an age
> I don't know, crying, let me see her again! —
> See her as she was, if that must be —
> See this last scene as it was, without a change,
> If that must be! But see her! Only a little!
> Once again! Before I go back!

Dag

> After this scene,
> The scene with Henry, I'll call her.

Richard

> Very well.
> Let's have him. (*He turns away. The lights dim on
>   Dag and Richard and come up on Henry and
>   his nobles in formal court costume.*)

HENRY   My friends and nobles, we
                     May breathe more easily now! The savage king
                     Who ruled here in this island, has been buried,
                     In the mud of a battlefield.
                     Richard the Third is dead. The bloody boar,
                     The guilty dog, is dead! Now you shall see
                     Justice instead of murder, gentleness
                     Instead of rape, the truth is open councils
                     Instead of falsehood. My first act has been
                     To redeem the name of Edward Fourth. His
                          children
                     Were not bastards, he was no bigamist,
                     As Richard proclaimed. And to do further
                          honour
                     To Edward's blood and line, I shall now make
                     Elizabeth, his daughter, queen of England,
                     By taking her to wife. Her mother, the widow
                     Of Edward Fourth, shall have a place in our
                          court,
                     Shall be queen mother. Elizabeth, is this
                     What you would choose?

ELIZABETH, SR.   Do you address me or my daughter,
                     My lord? We are both Elizabeth.

HENRY   I address
                     Your daughter first.

ELIZABETH, JR.   My lord, I have not wished
                     To marry, have not looked so high.

HENRY   But now,
                     Hearing the offer, does yes come to your lips,
                     Or no? You are free to choose.

ELIZABETH, SR.   Let me answer for her,
                     My dread lord. Before you offer marriage

	To my daughter, where are my sons?
HENRY	The guilty despot
	Who came before me, Richard, must answer
	that.
	Your sons are dead. He killed them.
ELIZABETH	They were alive
	After his death. I saw them alive and well
	After the battle of Bosworth.
HENRY	You mistake
	The date then.
ELIZABETH	I tell you I saw them! — If they are dead
	You killed them!
HENRY	No more at present.
	We shall have private conference. Bishop Morton,
	We come next to you. You shall be made
	Our archbishop of Canterbury, and inducted
	Within the year. Our further plans shall be
	Revealed tomorrow.
LORD STANLEY	My lord!
HENRY	No more today.
LORD STANLEY	My lord, I am sorry
	If I should seem importunate, but the lands
	That I was promised —
HENRY	You shall have all and more
	Than you were promised, Stanley; in my own
	time.
	This concludes the presence.
LORD STANLEY	*(Bowing.)* My lord.
HENRY	Save for Bishop Morton.
MORTON	Yes, my liege. *(The nobles and their ladies go out, bowing, leaving Morton and Polydore Vergil with Henry.)*

HENRY	I said alone!
MORTON	I have —
HENRY	Alone! *(Morton bows and Vergil goes out hastily.)*
	This queen mother woman, Elizabeth!
	This is not be borne! Take care of her!
MORTON	Quite easily, your grace.
HENRY	There are convents
	From which one hears nothing?
MORTON	There are.
HENRY	Keep her alive.
	It may be useful.
MORTON	Will you marry the daughter?
HENRY	I have no liking for it, but she is
	The daughter of Edward, and strengthens
	My tenuous title to this crown I wear.
MORTON	The boys are dead?
HENRY	They are. I had to make
	Elizabeth legitimate to piece out
	My claim to the succession. But that made
	The sons legitimate also. They were then
	The obvious heirs to the throne. Well, they are
	dead,
	And since the mother seems recalcitrant
	We'll place her where folk don't talk.
MORTON	Is that enough?
HENRY	What do you mean?
MORTON	A more elaborate story
	With names and dates and witnesses is needed
	If men are to be convinced.
HENRY	Convinced of what?
MORTON	That Richard killed them.
HENRY	I have a storm

            Of things to do. I have no time to fashion
            A story with witnesses and dates. Those Stanley
                brothers,
            Let them be placed where they can be forgotten
            And nothing said. As for the children, Richard,
            Their uncle, killed them!

MORTON   But your bare word, my lord,
            Will not be taken for this. Oh, at first it will,
            While it's not healthy to contradict. But later,
            The chroniclers will find you out.

HENRY   Well, let them.

MORTON   Let them?

HENRY   Can they be stopped?

MORTON   I think they'd better be.
            You wish to leave a Tudor name, to found
            A Tudor dynasty. But the Tudors have
            No claim to the throne.

HENRY   This is treason.

MORTON   In anyone else.
            To make it certain that no rebel ever
            Tries to put the Plantagenets back in power
            You must blacken your predecessor. Make him
                so foul
            That he's a by-word. Otherwise sometime
            Somebody will look too hard at your antece-
                dents,
            And find them flimsy, and stir people up,
                perhaps
            Overthrow you — or your son.

HENRY   Let us blacken him then.
            How do we go about it?

MORTON   In the first place,

It was Parliament put Richard on the throne,
Declaring him king after Edward. Expunge that
     act,
My lord, cut it out of the rolls. Make it appear
That he usurped his place.

HENRY   Who can do this?

MORTON   There are experts who know where to find the
     vellum
Clear back to the Conqueror. Give me power to
     do it
And I'll see it's done.

HENRY   You have it.

MORTON   That's to begin.
History's written by the victors, or
So the proverbs say. We'll write it. We'll em-
     ploy
Our own historians to indite our version
Of Richard's reign. If there's anything you've
     done
You'd rather not be blamed for, anything
That Edward did, that we could lay on Rich-
     ard,
Let's set our scriveners at it.

HENRY   Do you have men in mind?

MORTON   This lad that was here —
He's a historian of some note at home —
He can be paid to write.

HENRY   Can he be trusted?

MORTON   If we pay him enough.
Shall I call him?

HENRY   He's ready to begin?

MORTON   He has no honor, piety or truth,

	I've sounded him. Fear nothing. He's a writer.
	And the sooner we're launched the better.
	There's too much truth
	Abroad. It must be headed off with lies.
HENRY	Bring him. *(Morton steps to the door and beckons.*
	Vergil enters and bows.)
MORTON	You will make some notes of this.
VERGIL	Yes, monsignor.
MORTON	The murder of the princes, Edward's heirs,
	Was carried out by Richard. Dress that up
	With names and dates, and the kind of acces-
	sories
	That make gossip into truth.
VERGIL	Yes, truly. *(He bows over his notes.)*
MORTON	What else?
HENRY	He murdered Henry the Sixth! Why this is a
	game
	Such as I hadn't imagined! We'll write our own,
	Our very own history!
MORTON	And the world will take it!
HENRY	You have that?
VERGIL	Yes, my lord.
HENRY	He murdered Clarence!
	But wait, now, wait. Clarence was executed
	By Edward.
MORTON	We control the documents.
	That can be arranged.
HENRY	You're sure of that?
MORTON	Yes.
	We place new records where the old have lain,
	And truth lies darkling.
HENRY	Good! He murdered Clarence!

VERGIL	Could I suggest—?
MORTON	Yes?
VERGIL	Why, I've heard it said

That Clarence liked wine over-much. Just for a
       by-word
Let it be whispered about as Richard's jest,
"He was drowned in a butt of Malmsey."

HENRY	Vergil, your name is?
VERGIL	Yes, my lord. Polydore Vergil.
HENRY	I like this Vergil

Better than the other!

MORTON	I was right?
HENRY	Right. And now

I have an idea. This game gives me ideas.
This Richard lad was a slim young man-at-arms
Who took the fore-front in battles. I did well
To stay out of his reach. But when we write
       about him
Let us make him a monster. Let us make him
       hump-backed,
And lame! With a horrible aspect!

MORTON	And born with teeth!
HENRY	A full set!
VERGIL	And a head of hair!
HENRY	And a withered arm.

Two withered arms!

MORTON	No—one. One withered arm.
HENRY	Why one?
MORTON	Why, he fought in battles.

He held a sword.

HENRY	Very good. One withered arm. But, let me see,

Are there no pictures of Richard?

MORTON If there are

This story will destroy them! Who wants to believe

The dull truth when a horrid heap of bones

Comes mumbling and murdering out with a
 fee-fie-foe

And a withered arm? That's edged with genius,

That withered arm part! *(Richard moves slowly in
the shadows, and Henry, catching sight of
him, seems to realize his position.)*

HENRY I've been tricked again!

Fools! We've been tricked—you, too,

Morton of Ely—you with your Vergil!

No more of this!

MORTON My lord, what's wrong?

HENRY There's Richard in the shadows!

And that's the jury. Sitting there in rows!

A monstrous jury, sitting to judge of us

In some latter-day festival,

In a court unknown!

Say nothing! I'll say no more !

Go! *(Morton and Vergil dim and vanish, but Henry
cannot find the exit, and runs back and forth
against the curtains looking for it. Dag leaps
into the scene to stop him, and Richard, following, blocks the other side. Henry runs to
and fro like a ball-player trapped between
bases, dwindling in stature till he begins to
look like a rat again.)*

DAG Here! No—there he goes!

RICHARD He's here. No—the rat eludes me.

DAG Damn him! *(He catches Henry, then loses him.)*

RICHARD   He's got smaller!

DAG   He's turning back to rat!

RICHARD   *(Getting a firm grip on Henry's collar.)* I begin to
                    believe

               In the transmigration of souls! Pythagorus

               Understood these things!

HENRY   *(Snapping.)* Ck, ck, ck!

DAG   Don't let him bite you!

               It's poisonous! He's filthy!

RICHARD   He's bitten me already! *(He shakes Henry.)*

               I see it now, you very filthy king!

               A commoner,

               Not even a fanatic,

               With no excuse beyond a rat's ambition

               To break in among the sausages.

               You've worked

               From the beginning, to make yourself king of
                    England!

               A maker of sour music, king of England!

               First with Clarence, you plotted and connived,

               And kidnapped,

               Pretending he was to reign,

               Then with Hastings, saying he'd be king,

               Then with Stanley, letting him have illusions,

               But you'd have none,

               You meant it all for yourself!

               One by one you destroyed them, and went on,

               Murdering, lying, planning in secret,

               Till at last the throne was mine —

               And you could take it from me

               By promising Stanley what I wouldn't give him,

               Making a traitor of the man I trusted,

	And when you'd beaten me, when I was gone
	You cut off Stanley's head—and you were king!
	Go back to your part,
	Show yourself as the liar you were,
	And are, and should be in history!
	Go back to your part. *(He shakes Henry again.)*
HENRY	I will not!
DAG	No? *(He looks steadily at Henry.)*
HENRY	Let me go! Let go! *(He twists in Richard's grasp.)*
	Take your eyes from my face!
RICHARD	Go back and act your part!
	Bring in your shady advisors!
HENRY	*(Straightening a little.)* Why, if I must.
	If you must have it.
RICHARD	*(Letting go of Henry.)* Paugh! What an odor!
HENRY	*(Straightening still more.)* Yes!
	We'll act out the scenes if you like! It won't change
	The minds of the jury! Tell it as much as you like!
	Tell it and show it! The histories have stood
	Four hundred years the same! Men know what they think
	Of Richard and of Henry! You're a hunchback
	And a murderer of children!
RICHARD	I had no motive
	For murdering Edward's children, and you had!
HENRY	But do you think
	This will be believed? Our history is written
	By the survivors! As I remember it
	You did not survive! *(Al looks in, at stage right.)*
RICHARD	No, I did not!

But truth has power over error!
The men of today
Would rather believe the truth than your lies!
Here I stand,
A convicted murderer!
And the rat who won founded the Tudor line!
Those out front, will they let him go back and
      sleep
His gold-leaf sleep? And send me back to my
      rag-weed—
To thank God I have no hay fever?

AL   *(Who has been listening.)* If I may—

RICHARD   Speak, sir.

AL   I was out in the lobby tonight,
After the first act. I listened to the audience.
And the feeling was that though it was interest-
      ing
To see what happened,
And it might very well be true
That it happened this way,
They liked the old version better,
With its hump-backed usurper
And they'd rather watch it again,
Though it might be fiction,
Because it seemed bright and clear and real.

RICHARD   And we seem misty?

AL   Yes.

RICHARD   My memory of things is misty.
Compared with that scene we saw early in the
      evening
It's misty indeed.
Maybe when a great poet takes over history—

| | Whether it's lies or truth — and writes his vision |

Whether it's lies or truth — and writes his vision
Into such blazing words, that's reality —
What really happened has no chance against
    it. —
Beware of great poets, then.
What they say is final, can't be contradicted.
Well — let it go as it is!
Let the rat king lie down
Among his stolen purples! The poet wins.
His earth's more real than ours. Let me see
    Anne.
Dismiss old Henry. *(Henry fades, disappears.)*

DAG   I loved King Richard, I loved
My mistress. *(Al goes out.)*

RICHARD   Let that be enough.

DAG   My king,
I'm beaten.

RICHARD   *(putting an arm round Dag's shoulders)* We're beaten
    together,
My Dag and me. I'm sorry.

KENT   *(Walking on briskly from backstage.)*
All rights, ladies and gentlemen! The stage will
    be cleared and we'll proceed. You've had
    your time, you two.

RICHARD   We've had our time. *(Richard and Dag begin to
    fade. Three or four policemen follow Kent onto
    the stage.)*

KENT   Mr. Leger and I have decided that since it's
    grown so late we'll jump to the wooing of
    Elizabeth by Richard, if the audience
    doesn't object. The police and I will
    withdraw. *(He goes out with the police.*

*Richard and Dag are now barely perceptible.
The Player King enters, meeting Elizabeth, the
queen mother.)*

PLAYER KING   Stay madam. I must speak a word with you.

ELIZABETH   I have no more sons of the royal blood
For thee to murder.

PLAYER KING   You have a daughter called Elizabeth.

ELIZABETH   And must she die for this? Oh, let her live,
And I'll corrupt her manners, stain her beauty,
Throw over her the veil of infamy!

PLAYER KING   Wrong not her birth, she is of royal blood!

ELIZABETH   To save her life I'll say she is not so!

PLAYER KING   You speak as if that I had slain my cousins!

ELIZABETH   Cousins indeed, and by their uncle cozened
Of comfort, kingdom, kindred, freedom, life!

PLAYER KING   Look, what is done cannot be now amended.
If I have killed the issue of your womb,
To quicken your increase I will beget
Mine issue of your blood upon your daughter!

RICHARD   *(To Dag.)* But when do I see Anne?

DAG   *(To Richard.)* We've had our time.

RICHARD   You promised me that scene again!

DAG   I know.

AL   *(Prompting the Player King.)* "A grandam's name is
little less in love—"

PLAYER KING   A grandam's name is little less in love
Than is—I've forgotten again.

DAG   Call her. Call Anne.

RICHARD   Anne, did you call my name?

ANNE   *(Appearing faintly in the background.)* Oh, Richard,
Richard!
You were away so long!

AL	*(Prompting.)* "Than is the doting title —"
PLAYER KING	I can't go on!
RICHARD	So many things —
DAG	Begin again.
RICHARD	Anne, did you call my name?
ANNE	Oh, Richard, Richard, You were away so long!
RICHARD	I want to tell of my love! I want to use new words! *(Anne begins to fade.)*
ANNE	Richard, I saw your face — But now it darkens — *(She looks round her.)*
RICHARD	Anne —!
ANNE	Where am I?
RICHARD	Anne! Look at my face! *(She fades further.)* Here my voice only! We are alone, I shall not see you again, In all the world of worlds, and in all time I shall see you only now. And it was you Alone I loved. I never loved another. Look at me! Take my hand!
ANNE	You loved Elizabeth!
RICHARD	That was a lie. I loved you only, you only! You must hear me! Look at me! Take my hand!
ANNE	*(Brightening a little.)* You called me? You want me?
RICHARD	I want you only. Wanted you only, always.
ANNE	The darkness washes over me in a wave! I don't know where I am! Am I dying? Richard!

RICHARD   Take my hand. Look only at me. I love you.

It was not true I loved elsewhere.

ANNE   Richard, Richard,

You loved Elizabeth! It's all forgiven,

Forgotten! *(She dims.)*

RICHARD   Remember our Christmas time,

And our little son,

"Oh, red and jolly

Is the holly,

In the winter rime!"

ANNE   "Red and jolly," yes, that was the song

He sang with Dag at Christmas. *(Her face
       brightens.)*

I've been ill. Am I dying, Richard?

RICHARD   There was a lie

Told you when I was away, and I never saw
       you

To tell you it wasn't true. I loved you only.

Never loved Elizabeth. The woman lied.

ANNE   I think it would kill me

If it were true you loved elsewhere. I would die

Only hearing of it.

RICHARD   Sweetheart, you did die.

And I was away in battle, and could not see
       you

Till you were gone. And then I died at Bos-
       worth.

And we are both dead.

ANNE   Dead — and I see you?

RICHARD   By some magic word

And because of the great love that is in me

For you, and in you for me, we have this moment

Even though we are dust, long dust. For I must
    tell you
I loved you only.

ANNE   Richard. You loved me only?

RICHARD   You only.

ANNE   Then I am happy. Now I know
You called me from a long sleep.

RICHARD   Yes.

ANNE   I'm happy. I can be happy lying there
With our little son.

RICHARD   Smile once before you go
At Dag, who let this happen. He loves you too.

ANNE   *(Smiling at Dag.)* Dag, too. *(She looks round.)* But
    who are these?

RICHARD   No one that matters.

ANNE   Could I keep with you?

RICHARD   The spell won't hold for long.
I'll have to go. And lose you.

ANNE   But now I have you.
Forever.

RICHARD   Yes. As long as death lasts you have me.
And I have you. And that will be a long time.

DAG   A long time. *(The light fades on Richard and
Anne, and finally, on Dag. But before he
disappears Dag lifts an arm and beckons
for the curtain, which begins to come down.
While it is descending Al prompts the Player
King.)*

AL   "A grandam's name is little less in love —"

PLAYER KING   A grandam's name is little less in love —

Curtain

(After the curtain Kent enters from stage right, and Leger from stage left, in front of the curtain. Al follows Kent.)

KENT   Tomorrow evening we'll give *Richard Third!*

AL   I didn't take the curtain down, Mr. Leger. Shall I take it up?

LEGER   Let it go. We'll give *Richard Third* tomorrow.

The End

Notes to the Play
(by Roxane C. Murph)

Page 38, lines 3ff	Anderson cut many lines of the dialogue from Shakespeare's *Richard III,* having the characters of the Player King and Queen say just enough lines to give the sense of the scenes.
Page 44, lines 21–22	Richard and his wife, Anne Neville, were first cousins once removed. Anne's father, Richard, Earl of Warwick, was the brother of Richard's mother, Cecily Neville.
Page 45, lines 8–10	Richard was buried in the Grey Friars Monastery in Leicester, and his grave was marked by a simple monument erected by Henry VII a few years after the Battle of Bosworth. At the dissolution of the monasteries in 1536, during the reign of Henry VIII, the grave was destroyed and the bones thrown into the River Soar. The exact site of the grave is uncertain, since the monastery and its church no longer exist.
Page 58, lines 8–12	The "group of displaced paranoids" no doubt refers to the members of the Richard III Society, an international organization of people who believe in the innocence of Richard III, and who are dedicated to promoting research into his life and times.
Page 58, lines 26–28	Richard was married only once. It was Henry VIII who married several wives and disposed of them when they no longer suited his purposes.
Page 60, line 17 to Page 61, line 5	Richard went to live at Middleham, in the household of the Earl of Warwick, his cousin, at the age of nine, and remained until he was thirteen. It was a common practice at the time for a noble

family to send its sons to learn the knightly arts from other members of the nobility. Anne was about seven years old when Richard came to live at Middleham. In 1470, when Warwick rebelled against Edward IV and joined forces with Marguerite of Anjou to restore Henry VI to the throne, Anne was betrothed to Henry's son, Edward of Lancaster. They may, indeed, have been married, but it is almost certain the the marriage was never consummated, since Marguerite wanted her husband firmly seated on the throne before she would allow the daughter of the man she hated above all others to become her son's wife in fact.

Page 71, lines 6–8   Warwick died at the Battle of Barnet on April 14, 1471. This was Richard's first important battle, and he commanded the right wing of the Yorkist army. Anne at this time was still in France with Marguerite of Anjou and Edward of Lancaster, and they did not land in England until the day of the Battle of Barnet. On May 4, at the Battle of Tewkesbury, in which Richard commanded the left wing of his brother's army, Edward of Lancaster was either killed fleeing the battlefield or stabbed to death by Edward's nobles as he pleaded for his life with his brother-in-law Clarence. Chroniclers differ on this point. Marguerite and Anne were taken back to London as prisoners. Marguerite was finally ransomed by the French king, and Anne was given into the custody of Clarence. She did not return to Middleham until she and Richard married and went there to live. Neither Clarence nor Isabel was there at this time.

Page 72, line 5–6   Clarence deserted Warwick after their return from France, and went over to the king's side. The three brothers were reunited, and their combined forces defeated those of Warwick and his brother John, Marquis Montague, and both were killed.

Page 72, lines 27–28   Edward IV had given orders that Warwick's life
page 73, line 2   was to be spared, but his men were either ignorant of the order, or chose to ignore it. Warwick

and his brother were seized and slain as they attempted to flee the field.

Page 75, lines 7–8   Anne died in March 1485, probably of consumption (tuberculosis), a common killer of the time, and the disease which probably killed her sister Isabel as well. Anne was laid to rest in Westminster Abbey on the right hand side of the High Altar. In 1960 the Richard III Society installed a memorial tablet to mark her grave.

Page 95, lines 29– page 76, line 2   Sir George Buck, in his *The History of Life and Reigne of Richard III,* wrote that before Anne's death, Elizabeth of York, the daughter of Edward IV, had written a letter to the Duke of Norfolk, Richard's friend and supporter. She wrote that "she desires him [Norfolk] to be a mediator for her to the King, in the behalf of the Marriage propounded between them, who, as she wrote, was her only joy and maker in this world, and that she was his in heart and thought: withall insinuating that the better part of *February* was past, and that she feared the Queen would never die." Buck added that the letter, in Elizabeth's own hand, was then in the possession of Thomas, Earl of Arundel and Surrey (Norfolk's son). The letter is no longer extant. Buck noted further that Richard had no intention of marrying his niece, but had only entertained the idea out of policy, since he had not married her when he was free to do so after Anne's death (London: EP Publishing, 1973; reprint of 1647 edition, pages 128–129). The rumor to the effect that Richard would marry Elizabeth after Anne's death caused great uneasiness in England, since such a marriage was within the forbidden bounds of consanguinity. It is uncertain whether or not Richard ever had any such intention, or merely entertained the idea to forestall Henry Tudor, who had promised to marry the Yorkist princess. In any event, Richard, persuaded by his closest advisors, called together the mayor of London, the aldermen, and many of the nobility in the great hall of the Hospital of St. John, and denied that he ever had any intention of marrying his niece, and warned his audience to stop spreading such rumors, or suffer the consequences.

Page 76, line 18   Gules—the armorial tincture red, depicted on a shield by perpendicular lines.

Page 82, line 20   Richard's cognizance, or badge, was the white boar.

Page 82, line 24   Henry Tudor, who is referred to several times in this play as a music master, never held that position, or any other, at the court of Edward IV. He spent most of his adult life in exile in Brittany and France as a pensioner of their rulers. Although Edward IV and Richard III both made attempts to capture Henry, or lure him back to England, they were unsuccessful, and when Henry landed in Wales in August 1485, it was the first time he had set foot on British soil in fourteen years.

Page 83, line 4   Bishop John Morton of Ely, a Lancastrian, was a member of the council under both Edward IV and Richard III. He was arrested for treason on June 13, 1483, during the same council meeting in the Tower at which Hastings was arrested and executed. Morton was sent to Brecon Castle in Wales in the custody of the Duke of Buckingham. Shortly afterward Morton persuaded Buckingham to rebel against Richard, for the ostensible purpose of putting Edward V back on the throne. The rebellion failed, Buckingham was captured and executed, and Morton escaped to Flanders and thence to Brittany, where he joined Henry Tudor.

Page 85, lines 17–25   Clarence, who obtained the guardianship of Anne after the final defeat of the Lancastrians at Tewkesbury, was determined that she should not marry his brother Richard. He hid her in the London home of one of his retainers, where she was forced to work as a kitchen maid, until she was found and rescued by Richard. Neither Henry nor Morton was involved in the incident.

Page 95, lines 32–
page 96, line 3   At this period the steward was the head of the household, and was in charge of the rest of the staff, the position now held by the butler. The medieval butler was in charge of the wine cellar.

Page 99, lines 10–15   Clarence was arrested in 1478, many years after this incident, and after Isabel's death. Edward IV had endured much, including treason, from Clarence, but when the duke arrested and executed two of his late wife's servants on false charges, publicly accused the king of trying to destroy him, and spread the tale that Edward was the illegitimate son of an archer, he went too far. He was arrested, tried, found guilty of treason, and executed on February 18, 1478. Richard pleaded with Edward not to execute Clarence, but the queen and her family urged his death. Edward is said to have regretted his decision for the rest of his life.

Page 99, lines 32–
page 100, line 4   After Anne's rescue Richard took her to the sanctuary of St. Martin le Grand for safety. For several months afterward Richard and Clarence had a bitter and public dispute over Anne and her inheritance. Since Richard was eager to marry Anne, with or without her share of the Warwick estates, an agreement was finally reached. Anne came out of sanctuary and married Richard in the spring of 1472. They left immediately for Middleham, part of the Warwick property which Richard received in the settlement, and it was there that their only child, Edward, was born a year later.

Page 100, lines 13ff   Bishop Stillington of Bath and Wells informed Richard and members of the council that Edward IV had been contracted in marriage to Lady Eleanor Butler, the daughter of the Earl of Shrewsbury, before he married Elizabeth Woodville. In the eyes of the church a marriage contract was as binding as a marriage, and since Lady Eleanor was alive when Edward married Elizabeth Woodville, the marriage was considered bigamous and the children born of it illegitimate. It was for this reason that Richard claimed the throne.

Page 103, lines 9–19   At Richard's urging, Parliament passed several laws to reform abuses, which made him popular with the commons, if not with the nobility. Benevolences, a type of forced loan, were made illegal, and the first law to protect and encourage the printing of books in England was passed. Property laws to protect buyers from dishonest sellers, statutes to reform the machinery of justice, and the first statute of limitations were enacted. In addition the Parliament passed acts to protect the innocent from both oppression by officers of the law and malicious lawsuits, as well as one to ensure qualified juries in all trials. He reformed the machinery of government to make it more efficient, inaugurated the first mail service, and founded the College of Arms. For a good overview of the accomplishments as well as the problems of Richard's short reign, see Paul Murray Kendall's *Richard the Third* (New York: W.W. Norton, 1956, pages 370–391).

Page 103, lines 24–26   Anne and Richard's son Edward died at Middleham on April 9, 1484. "On hearing the news of this," wrote the Croyland chronicler, "at Nottingham, where they were then residing, you might have seen the father and mother in a state almost bordering on madness, by reason of their sudden grief" *(Ingulph's Chronicle of the Abbey of Croyland,* edited and translated by Henry T. Riley; London: Henry G. Bohn, 1854, pages 496–497).

Page 104, lines 20–24   Young Edward's last Christmas, which he celebrated at Middleham less than four months before his death, was not shared by Edward IV, his queen, their sons, or his parents. Richard and Anne were in London at this time, but their son was too ill to join them. By this time Edward IV had been dead for nearly eight months, Elizabeth Woodville was in sanctuary in Westminster, and Richard III was king.

Page 104, lines 25–26   Edward IV had chosen Richard to be protector on his deathbed, knowing that a strong leader would be needed to keep apart the warring factions of his court, and to guide the new young king until he reached his majority and was able to govern alone.

Page 110, lines 14–17   William the Conqueror landed in Pevensey on the English Channel, and went from there to Hastings where he defeated Harold.

Page 110, line 28   At this time monarchs as well as dukes and
                      duchesses were addressed as Your Grace. The
                      term Your Majesty did not come into use until
                      the reigns of the Tudors, who inaugurated it to
                      emphasize the distance between the throne and
                      the rest of the populace.

Page 111, line 13   Anne celebrated one more Christmas, but she was
                      by then terminally ill. She died on March 16,
                      1485, during an eclipse of the sun.

Page 112, lines 4ff   At the time of Edward IV's death Elizabeth
                      Woodville's brother Anthony, Lord Rivers, was
                      in Ludlow with her son, the new king, whom
                      he served as governor. They set out for Lon-
                      don as soon as they received word from Eliza-
                      beth, who was eager to have her son crowned
                      immediately, so that Richard of Gloucester could
                      be prevented from exercising his authority as
                      protector. Rivers and Sir Richard Grey, one
                      of Elizabeth's two sons from her first marriage,
                      met Richard at Northampton, where the protec-
                      tor arrested them. They were executed at Ponte-
                      fract shortly thereafter. Hastings was at this
                      time one of Gloucester's supporters, and Henry
                      Tudor was in exile in Brittany. When Elizabeth
                      realized that her plan to rule through her young
                      son had failed, she fled into sanctuary with her
                      children.

Page 121, lines 20ff Lord Stanley was Tudor's stepfather, and his
                      loyalty was always questionable. Although Rich-
                      ard knew that Margaret Beaufort, Stanley's wife,
                      was involved in Buckingham's rebellion, her hus-
                      band seems to have had the king's trust until just
                      before Bosworth. When Stanley refused to comply
                      with Richard's command to come to his aid with
                      an army, the king seized Lord Strange, Stanley's
                      son, as a hostage. During the battle Stanley and
                      his brother held back their men, waiting to see
                      which side would win. At the critical moment
                      they came in on Tudor's side, thus ensuring that
                      the victory went to him. Although Anderson
                      places Rivers and Grey in this scene, they were
                      both executed shortly after their arrest at North-

ampton in 1483, more than two years before the battle of Bosworth.

Page 124, lines 18ff Henry Tudor, supported by men and money from the French king, made his first attempt to invade England in October 1483, during Buckingham's rebellion. When he realized, however, that the uprising was a failure, he turned back to France to await a better opportunity.

Page 125, lines 20ff Lord Thomas Stanley had been given many of Buckingham's possessions and offices, including that of Lord Constable of England. Stanley's brother, Sir William, was appointed Chief Justice of North Wales, and Constable of the castle and Captain of the town of Caernarvon. Margaret Beaufort, who was deeply involved in Buckingham's plot, was deprived of her titles, but her lands were given to her husband for life. Stanley persuaded Richard to remit the attainder of his wife, and although she was put into the custody of her husband who was answerable for her good behavior, she remained free to continue her plotting in behalf of her son.

Page 130, line 5–9 This speech is reminiscent of the last scene of Shakespeare's *Richard III,* in which the victorious Henry, declaring that "the bloody dog is dead," promises "smiling plenty, and fair prosperous days" in England. His promise of justice, gentleness, and truth, in Anderson's words, were belied by his love of secrecy, his suspicion of virtually everyone except his mother and a few close advisors, and the fact that he employed an army of spies to ferret out any suspicion of treason. His avarice, and his genius for acquiring money from his subjects, made him both feared and disliked.

Page 130, lines 13–17 On Christmas day in 1483 Henry and his supporters met at the cathedral in Rennes in Brittany, where Henry swore that he would marry Elizabeth of York as soon as he became king. The delay in carrying out his promise, caused by the necessity of reversing the law stigmatizing her as illegitimate, caused much discontent among the English, who saw it as Henry's attempt to show

<table>
<tr><td></td><td>that he did not need the Yorkist heiress to strengthen his claim to the throne. The two were finally married on January 18, 1486.</td></tr>
<tr><td>Page 131, lines 1–12</td><td>From her actions during the reign of Richard III, Elizabeth Woodville did not appear to believe that the king had murdered her sons. She came out of sanctuary with her daughters and sent word to her son Dorset, who was with Henry in Brittany, that it was safe for him to return to England. She did, however, conspire with Margaret Beaufort, and agreed to marry her daughter Elizabeth to Henry, probably because she believed that she would be restored to a position of importance.</td></tr>
<tr><td>Page 131, lines 19–28</td><td>Henry rewarded his stepfather Lord Stanley by creating him Earl of Derby, constable of England, and chief steward of the duchy of Lancaster, and by giving him grants of lands and manors. Sir William Stanley became chamberlain of the household and the exchequer, retained the offices in Wales that he had held under Richard III, and received as well large grants of land. In 1495, however, he lost everything, including his life, when he was discovered to be implicated in the Perkin Warbeck rebellion.</td></tr>
<tr><td>Page 132, lines 4–11</td><td>In 1487, when Henry learned of the plot instigated by Richard's nephew, the Earl of Lincoln, and Frances Lovell to place the pretender Lambert Simnel on the throne, he became suspicious that Elizabeth Woodville was implicated. He deprived her of her property and gave it to his wife, and sent her to the convent of Bermondsey, where she lived on a pension until her death on April 10, 1492.</td></tr>
<tr><td>Page 132, lines 16–22</td><td>Several candidates for the murderer of the princes have been suggested by professional and amateur historians in the past. While Richard III remains the favorite, both Buckingham and Henry Tudor have their accusers. Those who believe Richard innocent of the crime argue that he had no motive, since they had been declared illegitimate and thus barred from the succession. Many of these same people believe that Buckingham is the most</td></tr>
</table>

likely culprit, since he had both motive (he was descended from Edward III and may have fancied the role of king more than that of kingmaker) and opportunity, as he was Constable of the Tower and thus had access to it at all times. In addition, he remained in London for several days after Richard and Anne went on progress, and could have had the boys killed, hoping that their deaths would be blamed on the king. There are some who believe, as Anderson apparently did, that the boys were not killed until Henry came to the throne, and that he destroyed them to protect his position. And, of course, many people during the intervening centuries have believed that they were not murdered at all, but sent secretly either to the north of England or to the Continent, to emerge a few years later as one or both of the pretenders to the throne who plagued Henry in the early years of his reign.

Page 132, line 27– page 135, line 12

The so-called "Tudor Myth" had several sources, and was indeed the result of a conscious effort to give legitimacy to Henry's claim to the throne by blackening his predecessor's reputation. John Rous, a chaplain at Guy's Cliffe in Warwickshire, was the only contemporary Englishman to formulate some of the more outrageous charges against Richard III. Rous was a time-server who had praised Richard during his lifetime and vilified him after his death, describing his monstrous appearance at birth and accusing him of several murders. Bernard André, the tutor of Henry's son Arthur, added to the story, but it is generally Polydore Vergil who gets most of the credit, or blame, for institutionalizing the official version. Vergil, an Italian, came to England in 1502 as a collector of the papal tax known as Peter's Pence. In 1507 Henry asked him to write a history of England, and he was given access to many manuscripts and records, which he used in addition to printed sources. There is no question that he was biased, but the accusations made against him that he destroyed documents which disputed his version of events may be exaggerated. His *Anglica Historia,* which contained twenty-six books and covered English history from its beginning until 1509, the year of Henry's death, was published in 1534. The work embellished Rous' portrait of Richard as an unnatural monster, adding several murders to the score.

Thomas More's *History of Richard the Third* is, without doubt, the most important of the early works which gave us the picture of Richard III that most people accept today. More, who grew up in Archbishop Morton's household, no doubt absorbed many of the opinions of his mentor, and some will argue that the *History* is Morton's work and not More's, but this is unlikely. Kendall wrote that "the gross inaccuracies of this work, its apparently willful distortions of fact and its urgent bias, are not nearly so surprising as the positive virulence which informs it. Richard is entirely re-moved from the sphere of human life; he is evil incarnate, sheer monster, and as such he is re-viled" (*Richard III,* page 500). More's work was reprinted in the Tudor chronicles, notably those of Hall and Holinshed, Shakespeare's main sources for his history plays. It is therefore More's picture which Shakespeare gave us, but even more vividly and dramatically, and the one which most people, including those in the audience in *Richard and Anne,* prefer to any revisionist view. The Duke of Marlborough is said to have remarked, "I never read history. The only history I've ever learned, I learned from Shakespeare." It is true, as Richard says in this play, that when a great poet takes over history, whether it is lies or truth, it becomes reality.

Index to the Characters in the Play